THE
GENEROSITY
JOURNEY

THE
GENEROSITY
JOURNEY

GREG LOCKE

Global Vision Press ™

CHARISMA
HOUSE

THE GENEROSITY JOURNEY by Greg Locke
Published by Charisma House, an imprint of Charisma Media
1150 Greenwood Blvd., Lake Mary, Florida 32746
In association with Global Vision Press and Locke Media
2060 Old Lebanon Dirt Road, Mount Juliet, Tennessee 37122

Unless otherwise noted, all Scripture quotations are taken from the King James Version of the Bible.

Scripture quotations marked ESV are from The ESV® Bible (The Holy Bible, English Standard Version®), copyright © 2001 by Crossway, a publishing ministry of Good News Publishers. Used by permission. All rights reserved.

While the author has made every effort to provide accurate, up-to-date source information at the time of publication, statistics and other data are constantly updated. Neither the publisher nor the author assumes any responsibility for errors or for changes that occur after publication. Further, the publisher and author do not have any control over and do not assume any responsibility for third-party websites or their content.

For more resources like this, visit MyCharismaShop.com and the author's website at lockemedia.org.

Cataloging-in-Publication Data is on file with the Library of Congress.
International Standard Book Number: 978-1-63641-404-1
E-book ISBN: 978-1-63641-405-8

1 2024
Printed in the United States of America

Most Charisma Media products are available at special quantity discounts for bulk purchase for sales promotions, premiums, fund-raising, and educational needs. For details, call us at (407) 333-0600 or visit our website at www.charismamedia.com.

The author has made every effort to provide accurate accounts of events, but he acknowledges that others may have different recollections of these events.

DEDICATION

THE BIBLE IS very plain when it comes to the principle of taking care of widows. Both the Old and New Testaments teach us that God's blessing resides upon those who honor widows. I've had the privilege of pastoring a dear woman of God and widow named Patricia Caparas McKeown, who is now in the presence of the Lord. She served as one of the proofreaders for my books for a very long time, and she spent her final days on this earth helping bring this very book to press. She deeply loved Jesus, and she certainly loved her pastor, so I know the words and Scriptures in this book brought her great peace and encouragement as she prepared to see the Lord.

Our church began paying all the mortgages for our widows several years ago, and it was Patricia the Lord used to help me see the importance of such a decision. She will be greatly missed, but her legacy of kindness and generosity will live throughout eternity. This book is affectionately dedicated to her. I also want to recognize a gift she gave me that went beyond her faithful generosity to the church. It was the sacrifice of allowing her son, Wayne Caparas, and his beautiful wife, Lori, who cared for her, to be the spearheads and overseers of Locke Media and Global Vision Press even during her decline. Thank you, Patricia, for the life you lived, the lives you touched, and the people you left with us to build the kingdom of God.

CONTENTS

FOREWORD

As a recognized voice with a war cry to a generation, my friend, pastor, and cultural reformer Pastor Greg Locke takes us on a journey as only he can. Extravagant generosity is a hallmark of his ministry and lifestyle; therefore, he qualifies to write this book from a position of authority. I have witnessed his radical generosity on multiple occasions. If anything, my friend's actions to help others and display biblical giving far supersede the stories he shares in this book. He and his wife, Tai, are tremendous examples of the principles you will discover while reading the pages ahead.

Please think about this: How you handle kingdom economics will play a role in what you may be doing—and responsible for—in eternity. As Pastor Locke eloquently states, "Having more money will never make you a better steward. That's one of the biggest lies that's ever been told in Christianity." Followed by another important statement: "All God has given us now is for that—it's for now." Such refreshing insights! Especially when we look around today's culture and realize there is an alarming trend of influencers and even ministries committed to building shrines for themselves rather than storing up riches that will last for eternity.

An eternal mindset does not come to you without effort. Rather, anyone wanting to break out and start walking in God's economy can expedite the process by becoming generous. That means more than being a giver, going beyond the reasonable service of tithing and stepping into radical generosity. It will change everything for you!

This might sound controversial, but if you become radically generous, you will find favor in far more areas than you even deserve, all because you are engaging in a system God created for His people's benefit. You will start walking in a completely unfair advantage, but the beautiful thing is that it only really works if your heart is connected to the Lord and His Word while doing it. Generosity is not effective for transactional, self-serving individuals; it is effective for those who do it from the heart with cheerfulness—after all, God loves a cheerful giver!

Pastor Locke, a master of his craft, portrays this so well, and now you have the opportunity to glean from the revelatory gems and gold mine of insights you have in your hand. If you read this book with your heart, not just your head, the potential to unleash some yoke-busting horsepower will likely start manifesting in your life for the glory of Jesus!

One phrase in this book caught my attention because, with my mind's ear, I can hear Pastor Locke's voice nearly breaking into tears saying it: "There is nothing that will change your life more than biblical generosity...nothing." It is my persuasion that radical generosity is not only an act of worship but also a hidden secret that God is very watchful over. It's as if the Lord says, "Who of you will hear the cry of My heart?" For He so loved the world, He gave—beyond what anyone has ever given. The great delight of His heart was given on behalf of all humanity.

I applaud Pastor Locke for writing this timely and highly biblical approach to walking in generosity. If there were a lever pulled every time someone sowed in an outrageous fashion, my friend busted it. The results so far have been an ongoing revival, reaching America with one of the highest-rated Christian movies in its genre and countless people being delivered from the power of demonic activity. Pastor Locke is currently expanding what the Lord has given him and Tai to accomplish. All this is the fruit of radical generosity, because if what people sow doesn't mean much to them, neither will their harvest.

To my friend Pastor Greg Locke, thank you for allowing the Lord to use your life. So many captives have been set free, and the fires are only beginning to burn. I know this book will be a blessing and offer liberty for many.

For Jesus...

—JOSEPH Z
AUTHOR, BROADCASTER, PROPHETIC VOICE
JOSEPHZ.COM

INTRODUCTION

You will be enriched in every way to be generous in every way, which through us will produce thanksgiving to God.
—2 CORINTHIANS 9:11, ESV

A COUPLE OF YEARS before starting my three-book Spiritual Warfare Series, God said to me, "I'm going to give you a Saul-to-Paul Damascus Road experience, and I'm going to open your eyes like a little puppy to show you that the kingdom of God is not in *words* but in demonstration and in power of the Spirit." (See 1 Corinthians 2:4). My ensuing conversion is well documented in my books and in our hit theatrical film, *Come Out in Jesus Name*, so if you've been following us for a while, you probably know it well.

As I've reflected on this amazing turn of events and the

1

continual overflow of God's blessings that has accompanied them, I've often had to stop and ask the Lord, "Why me?"

Millions of believers and unbelievers alike have come to know our story, but I've never discussed the answer to that simple, timeless question—until now. It's important that I do so here in the introduction to *The Generosity Journey*, because it also answers why God would choose me to write a book about such an avoided yet crucial topic, and exactly why this book is so desperately needed in the body of Christ today.

First, I have always been a *Word* man, and there's no doubt that my intense love for the Bible started me on this journey while still just a teen. After all my years of Baptist seminary and more than a decade of on-the-job training as a traveling evangelist, I was *all Word all the time*, but the supernatural workings of the Spirit and the scriptures that clearly define them seldom hit my radar.

To prepare for the writing of this book, I was inspired to consume the Bible cover to cover in just one month, and to challenge our church to do the same. I had only accomplished this *one month* effort a single time in my entire life, just after being saved at the age of seventeen, and I knew it was time to do it again with my fresh forty-seven-year-old eyes.

In the four and a half months since throwing down that challenge, I'm grateful to report that I just completed my eighteenth pass. Yes, I had to weave in a lot of audiobook time to get here, but faith comes by hearing (Rom. 10:17), so that made it all the more powerful for me. You can trust that this book contains the fresh revelation that can only come from this sort of all-in consumption of God's holy Word.

Through these fresh readings, I also paid very close

attention to God's commands dealing with our supernatural demonstrations of power—especially as they relate to our giving. For those of you who don't know my conversion story, I was taught that all the supernatural workings of God through the people of God ceased when the original apostles died, so for most of my life I've been a cessationist's cessationist. I even wrote a book that vilified Charismatics, people who still believe we have supernatural power from God. Now look at me.

Saul to Paul indeed. It's still hard to believe that a Word man like me spent so much of my life explaining away the Word, but once I truly opened my eyes and repented, God's purposes for my life began to come into focus—even more so following these past eighteen readings.

Second, God gifted me with a generous heart from the very beginning, and He birthed that heart through my intense love for His Word. Please note that I don't demonize my past as a devout Baptist. I think this book and even this introduction will make that clear. My Baptist upbringing and training gave me a love for the Word that supercharged my generous heart, as it is without question a scriptural prerequisite regardless of whether you are a cessationist or a charismatic.

As I've allowed my generosity to mark the peaks and valleys of my life, every significant blessing along my journey has been a direct result of a personal act of sacrificial (sometimes extravagant) giving. This book explains how and why God did that for me. The massive media platform, the bestselling books, the hit movie, and especially the ongoing revival at Global Vision Bible Church—every good fruit of blessing—have all come on the heels of our extreme generosity to those in need.

We'll discuss *sowing and reaping* throughout this book, as it is a fundamental law of God. You can be sure I would never have been so blessed in this season had I not been so generous in prior seasons. For this, if you're looking for a breakthrough in *any* area of your life, you've picked up the right book. You will indeed be "enriched in every way" when you are generous in every way—in the right spirit.

As a Bible preacher, I have to make it clear that the mission the Lord has given me starts and ends with the authority of the Word of God. But after thirty years of preaching it, I need to remind you that the Holy Trinity is not God the Father, God the Son, and God the *Holy Bible*. Instead, it is God the Father, God the Son, and God the *Holy Spirit*. Through the written Word of the Bible, God Himself has taught me that the Holy Scriptures mean nothing without the illumination and revelation of the Holy Spirit, because no prophecy is of any private human interpretation—but only through the Spirit of God (2 Pet. 1:20).

Every word of God is for our learning and admonition (1 Cor. 10:11), so I'm right to call out the cessationist side for quenching the Spirit in their churches, just as I'm right to come to the charismatic side and say, "Cut out the foolishness and preach the Bible!" Even more, I'm right to call out both sides for their abominable lack of teaching on the laws of generosity, so buckle up.

The power of the Holy Spirit is still alive and at work in the church today, but as you'll learn, most Christians lack access due to their lack of obedience. People can indeed get healed and delivered and get their socks blessed off in every way possible, but there is a cost. The supernatural absolutely still happens, and there really is more in the Bible—even right there in the red letters of Jesus—than most of us have been taught. These are all significant themes of this book, and as you gain greater understanding (maybe even revelation) from the scriptures we'll unpack, I believe you're going to be drawn closer to Jesus in every way.

Since embracing the gifts of the Spirit, I've made a lot of new friends in the charismatic world, and I've been publicly criticized for befriending several of them—none more so than Benny Hinn. People on social media had a meltdown when I crossed that bridge. Two decades ago I wrote a book harshly criticizing the guy, so I get it, but that was then. Benny Hinn has since owned his past, and he's a far different preacher today than he was when I wrote that book. Even more, I was wrong for how I approached my criticisms, and I've apologized for it. We've both grown immensely since those days.

Today we're dear friends, and we talk frequently. He recently called me and said he heard I was going to be back in Orlando, and he wanted me to come to one of his crusades to do deliverance. Imagine that. Former Benny Hinn hater, former Baptist cessationist extraordinaire Greg Locke casting out demons at a Benny Hinn crusade. You can't make this stuff up.

While at the conference, I was sitting on the platform with a wide array of charismatic preachers who were among Benny's guests when he said something that points directly to my "Why me" question. While looking over at all of them, he said, "Let me tell you something about this young man sitting beside you. He knows the Bible better than all of you combined." And I was like, "Oh, dear Pastor, not now, please." You can imagine my discomfort.

Then Benny turned around and said to me, "Son, if I had to do it all over again, I would take your journey. I would start out as a Baptist so I could know the Bible like you, then get baptized in the Holy Spirit and tear the whole charismatic world up."

I was the least likely person to know anything about the charismatic world until God ripped me out of my Baptist comfort zone and placed me right in the middle of it all. He did this not just to make me a massive charismatic but to bring truth and balance to a movement that lacked both. Let's be honest. The charismatic world has been known for a lot of strange fire over the years, especially when money and materialism were involved, and God has not been pleased with it. Now that I've stood on both sides of the spectrum, I see what the Lord is doing with me.

He took me out of a movement that was all truth and no spirit and thrust me into a movement that was all spirit and very little truth. First the Lord raised up my platform. Then He said, "Let me tell you what your job is, Son. Preach spirit *and* truth to *all* the church—preach My heart—and help them finally see why I've given them so much." I believe the Lord raised up my ministry for such a time as this to say, "You know what? We want to see the miracles, signs, wonders, and especially the masses of salvations that marked the Acts church in the Bible, but we also want to see the *selfless* generosity that made it all flourish."

I know influential pastors on both sides who couldn't cast a demon out of a poodle and couldn't successfully pastor an outhouse, but they have ten thousand people in their church and millions of dollars in the bank. They run massive Christian-lite social clubs, and they're simply the main attraction. Meanwhile, very few of their people truly study the Bible, and even fewer obey God's commands. These ministries are a cancer in the body of Christ and a disgusting joke to the lost and dying world we're called to reach. God sees them the same way (Rev. 3:16).

If we can get the church back in balance, in spirit and in truth—starting with our biblical generosity toward others— we can change all of that in an instant. I'll revisit this later, but brace yourself for a shocking statistic: less than 2 percent of Christians obey the commands of biblical generosity, and that holds true on both sides of the church—cessationists and charismatics alike. Meanwhile, most of the failures in the church and in our personal lives can be traced back to this single tragic shortfall. After all, where your money is, there your heart will be also (Luke 12:34). Knowing that God requires 100 percent of our hearts, is it any wonder why the body of Christ is so lukewarm and demonized in these last of the last days?

I think the Lord wants people to understand that it's time for the body of Christ to quit playing games and simply obey the Bible—especially where generosity is concerned. God is thinning out the ranks and raising up an army, and He wants people who will lay down the selfish, lukewarm, casual approach to the Bible and simply obey, in spirit and in truth.

You could say this is a book about the eternal heaven-or-hell impact of obedience to the Word of God. The modern church certainly lacks sound teaching of this type. But you could also say it is a book about the overwhelming super-natural blessings of God that overflow from such obedience— on earth as in heaven—as well as its converse. This sort of teaching is also sorely lacking, and I hope *The Generosity Journey* starts a new trend across the full spectrum of the body of Christ.

While I believe my personal journey will inspire you to greater boldness, once you find your on-ramp onto your own personal generosity journey, I know a harvest of blessing awaits you in due season. Something supernatural happens when you finally put your money where your mouth is. When God can trust you to walk in biblical generosity, He will bless you beyond your imagination. As this book will prove, it really is that simple.

> By this we know love, that he laid down his life for us, and we ought to lay down our lives for the brothers. But if anyone has the world's goods and sees his brother in need, yet closes his heart against him, how does God's love abide in him? Little children, let us not love in word or talk but in deed and in truth.
> —1 John 3:16–18, esv

CHAPTER 1

THE JOURNEY BEGINS

W HEN I WAS a teen, God changed my life with His written Word, the Holy Bible. Many of you know I grew up in a children's home just forty miles from Global Vision Bible Church where I penned this book and am privileged to pastor. I was saved at the home, called to preach there, went off to Bible college from there, and still have deep-rooted connections to Good Shepherd Children's Home in Murfreesboro, Tennessee.

I had been saved for about two years when my pastor at the children's home, Dr. Tom Wallace, got up during a Wednesday night service and told us he would be going on a trip to Mexico the following week for a missions conference. I was eighteen at the time, and I remember saying to myself, "I don't have a passport, but I've got to go on that trip to Mexico." I'd never been out of the country at that time, unless you count West Virginia, so I asked the man of God if there was any way we could make it happen.

Dr. Wallace had a way of making things happen, and I'm blessed to say he is still a dear friend of mine in the ministry today. When I first approached him about the trip, it felt like I was making an impossible request, but it was no big deal for Pastor Tom. He said, "You know what? I think I can expedite you a passport and get you there," and that's exactly what he did. He did some finagling, called some officials, and somehow worked it all out. Before I knew it, I was on a four-seater airplane with my pastor and the chairman of the deacons on our way to Cuernavaca, Mexico.

This was the first time I had ever flown, and as we were taking off, I remember asking God why He was sending me to Mexico. I was just a kid on the greatest adventure of my young life, and that was overwhelming enough for me, but somehow I knew something was going to happen that would change everything about the way I see God and the world.

At the missions conference, I heard message after message from multiple speakers in a bilingual format. It was a no-frills, meat-and-potatoes conference, and I was riveted the entire time. But it was something that happened on the very last day that started me on the journey that is the subject of this book.

A SEMINAL MESSAGE

A Baptist preacher by the name of J. C. House was teaching, and right out of the gate he spoke twelve words that have become the seminal message of my entire ministry. I'll never forget it. He had on a dapper blue suit and a red tie. A distinguished-looking man, he honestly looked more like a sleek politician than a dressed-up pastor, but what he said set my course for the theological roller-coaster ride of my life.

Keep in mind, I was just an eighteen-year-old kid in a foreign land for the first time, about as far out of my element as I ever have been and still wondering when that life-changing moment was going to happen—or if it was even going to happen as I had anticipated. And suddenly out of J. C.'s mouth came that twelve-word phrase: "There is nothing that will change your life more than biblical generosity."

I must say, as an immature teenager whose past was a mess, it really doesn't even make sense why that message would wreck me the way it did—but it did. When he said that short phrase, it felt like a lightning bolt of the grace of God shot down from heaven and jolted me. It literally shook me to my core. That claim, on that night in Mexico, changed my life.

Today I can speak to you as living proof: there is nothing—no, nothing—that will change your life more than biblical generosity.

When J. C. House reached the end of his message, a man named Mike Patterson got up to take the offering. At the time he was the head of what is now called Mount Abarim Baptist Mission International. Mike said, "We're going to take an offering tonight from all the American preachers and their folks that are here, and we're going to take pledges from your churches to help us build churches and orphanages here in Mexico." As I sat there on the edge of my chair, it struck me deeply that I *lived* in an orphanage at the time.

Suddenly, a pastor stood up and said, "Our church will give $1,000." And everybody was like, "Yeah, amen." I had been taking notes the entire conference, so I wrote that down in my notebook: "Whoa...$1000 just like that, and they may never see the people who are blessed by it...pretty cool." Then a little lady jumped up and said, "I'll give $50." And everybody said amen and clapped. Then some preacher stood up and said, "Our church will give $10,000." And everybody was like, "Woohoo! Amen!"

It was super exciting to witness, and suddenly the Holy Spirit spoke to me. Remember, I'm just an eighteen-year-old kid who lived in an orphanage. I didn't even have a job, but the Holy Spirit said, "I want you to stand up and pledge $500."

Prior to when I got saved at seventeen, I had been such a delinquent that I was five years behind in school. Five full years. I hadn't even really started my education yet, and I didn't have any money at all. I wasn't even mowing grass at the time, so I had no clue where I would get the money. But God said, "Stand up, and out of your mouth verbally pledge that you're going to go home and send back $500." So I stood up and said, "Uh, I'll give $500."

And the place was pretty much silent. Everybody was like, "Whaaat?" If you're one of those people who think I don't look my age, you should have seen me at eighteen. Those folks were looking at me like I was a little kid wearing diapers, thinking, "Does his mama know he got on a plane and flew this far from home?"

There I was, just this skinny little nerdy-looking kid who stood up and stuck his neck where it had never been. Wanting to fill the silence, I quickly followed up by asking, "How long do I have to get it to you?" When they said they needed it in less than a month, I sat down thinking, "I have lost my mind."

LONG FLIGHT HOME

On the plane ride home, I kept going back over that impulsive moment, still not having a clue why the Lord would compel me like that and even wondering if I heard correctly—or whether it was just some bad burritos talking. At that age, I had not even seen $500 at one time. So I just kept thinking, all the way home, "Where in the world am I going to get $500?" It was a definite "Help me, Holy Ghost" moment. Long story short, He indeed helped me. I started mowing grass and putting aside every dollar possible.

More importantly, I started praying, "Lord, give me extra money somehow, someway. Let it come in the mail, let it come from places I could never expect it." I even called my mom and asked if she could give me $100 on Visitor Sunday at the children's home. I did whatever I could to keep my word, and somehow or other, over the course of three weeks, God provided the $500.

When I was finally able to sow that $500 into the mission, as a wide-eyed teenager, I was forever transformed. What that single month of my life did for me then is what it's still doing for me now. It lit a fire of stewardship and generosity in me that burns brighter today than ever. It forever proved to me that J. C. House's twelve-word axiom is true for all of us. There is nothing that will change your life more than biblical generosity. Nothing.

The journey that began for me in Cuernavaca, Mexico, has had some amazing and heart-stopping twists and turns along the way. Some put me on the global map as a preacher, some put me onto Facebook as a firebrand, and some are still playing out in movie theaters and bookstores around the world, but all put me firmly on my face at the feet of Jesus through acts of love for God and the "least of these" (Matt. 25:40).

Many of these experiences have opened my heart and mind to divine inspiration and revelations that still bring tears to my eyes and drive me to my knees, and everything I have accomplished in my life that has produced lasting fruit can be directly attributed to the Bible passages and inspirational stories we will discuss in this book. Whether you've been on this journey as long as me or are still looking for your own personal on-ramp, I pray this little book helps you set an ever-higher trajectory in your own generosity journey.

> Then the righteous will answer him, saying, "Lord, when did we see you hungry and feed you, or thirsty and give you drink? And when did we see you a stranger and welcome you, or naked and clothe you? And when did we see you sick or in prison and visit you?" And the King will answer them, "Truly, I say to you, as you did it to one of the least of these my brothers, you did it to me."
> —JESUS (MATTHEW 25:37–40, ESV)

AN UNHEALTHY OBSESSION

Twelve years after that initial trip to Mexico, right before we started Global Vision Bible Church, I was a part of the pastoral staff at a church in Murfreesboro, Tennessee, when I heard another profound statement about giving and generosity, and it too revolutionized me.

As I sat in the office of a superior in that ministry, I could hardly believe my ears. The man sat up in his chair, pulled his glasses down over his nose, and said in an overly authoritarian tone, "Let me tell you something, Greg Locke..." Now, from his demeanor, I knew what would proceed next from his mouth was not going to be positive. He said, and I quote, "You have an unhealthy obsession with giving money away." And I thought to myself, "Probably. In man's wisdom, anyway."

Though his counseling that day was intended as a rebuke, I can tell you that it steeled my resolve even as I submitted to his authority on that campus. When I get to the judgment seat of Christ, I'm not going to say, "Oh my goodness, Lord, I'm so sorry I gave so much away. Wilt Thou ever forgive me?" No. Instead, I will fall on my face and say, "Lord, I am so unworthy to be in Your presence. I gave so little. I did so little for You. I gave such a tiny, insignificant portion in comparison to every drop of blood You shed for me on Calvary."

I wouldn't want to approach the judgment seat only to give an account driven by the words that came out of this man's mouth that day. I was either going to back down as he suggested, or I was going to mash the gas. I chose the latter. On that day I realized that the church in America has an unhealthy obsession with being stingy and giving no money away, and two decades later it's truer than ever.

Most people say, "Oh, I'm a giver." But if you check their records, not only are they not giving, but there is usually little to no sacrifice in their life at all. Have you ever heard the phrase "I'm just going to give till it hurts"? Hardly anyone has ever truly done that. The church in America is stingy and greedy, period. Let's talk about that.

100 PERCENT TRUE OR 100 PERCENT LIE

I have shewed you all things, how that so labouring ye ought to support the weak, and to remember the words

of the Lord Jesus, how he said, It is more blessed to give
than to receive.

—ACTS 20:35

The Gospel writer Luke might have penned those words,
but it was the apostle Paul who was quoting the Lord. I find
it a fascinating bit of Bible trivia that neither of these men
were present when Jesus actually spoke the famous quote "It
is more blessed to give than to receive," but they were the
ones God chose to write them in stone. So let's make sure
we realize that is a red-letter quote, right out of the mouth
of Jesus.

What makes this famous quote so unique is that it was
never recorded in Matthew, Mark, Luke, or John, though it
can be argued that the Book of Acts is actually part two of
Luke's Gospel, so this is excellent historical evidence that
Jesus said and did far more than the Gospels ever recorded,
just as John claims in John 21:25.

When we drill into Jesus' words in that verse, we have to
realize it's either 100 percent true or 100 percent lie. It is either
more blessed to give than to receive or Jesus (and Paul under
Holy Ghost inspiration) made that up because He needed filler
words in the Bible. But know this, politicians may use gobble-
dygook and filibuster with empty words, but God never does.
God talks to change your life. And the reality of being more
blessed to give than to receive is one of the most life-altering
principles, laws, and phrases you will ever attempt to live by.

Thirty years removed from that fateful trip to Mexico at
the age of eighteen, I'm grateful to say I've been able to main-
tain a friendship with J. C. House, and I certainly never forgot
his words. That $500 absolutely changed my ministry path
and every fiber of who I am. Today it would be easy to look

back and say, "Well, you know, $500, that's not that big a deal." But at that moment it was like parting the Red Sea for me to stand up and pledge so much, let alone raise it.

At the time it truly seemed to be the most irresponsibly reckless thing I could have done. But the problem in the American church—other than the fact that it's far too American and not enough church—is that we play things so safe and measured. We're never reckless with our faith because we're taught by men that recklessness is loose faith. I'm writing this book to correct that. You cannot be too reckless with your faith. People say, "There's a fine line between faith and foolishness." And I say that it's *so* fine it's nonexistent.

> But the natural man receiveth not the things of the Spirit
> of God: for they are foolishness unto him: neither can he
> know them, because they are spiritually discerned.
> —1 Corinthians 2:14

The only people who say faith can be foolish are people who have no faith. Show me one person in the Bible that wasn't foolishly faithful (in man's sight) when they boldly stood up for the things of God. Jesus was the one who said, "You can say to this mountain, be removed and cast yonder into the sea, and it will be done" (see Mark 11:22–24). It's in red letters, so that sort of thinking is not foolish—it's the stuff of real faith.

CHAPTER 2

YOU DON'T HAVE A MONEY PROBLEM

WHEN IT COMES to personal giving, I know many of you may be thinking, "Oh, no, let me debate that with you, Pastor, so I can tell you about my financial realities." Please forgive me when I say I don't want to hear about your money woes. We all have them. Even Jesus had them. In reality, you don't have a money problem, you have a faith problem. I don't have money problems. I have faith problems. Churches don't have money problems. They have faith problems. Faith and stewardship are like conjoined twins. They are interconnected, and you cannot disconnect them. It takes faith to believe and operate in what I want to talk about, so buckle up.

GOD GAVE

> For God so loved the world, that he gave his only begotten
> Son, that whosoever believeth in him should not perish,
> but have everlasting life.
>
> —JOHN 3:16

God has a lot to say about giving, and here's why. The Bible
plainly says in John 3:16, "For God so loved the world that
He..." What's the next word? He didn't beg. He didn't borrow.
He didn't take. He didn't steal. He *gave*. Therefore, the very
nature of our God is the nature of giving. He gave us the sun
and moon and stars and this world and every single thing in
it that keeps us alive. He gave us our very lives, the breath
in our lungs, and every promise of the ever after. And to do
that He gave us Jesus Himself as a gift only He could give,
through a sacrifice only He could make.

> Yet it pleased the LORD to bruise him; he hath put him to
> grief: when thou shalt make his soul an offering for sin,
> he shall see his seed, he shall prolong his days, and the
> pleasure of the LORD shall prosper in his hand.
>
> —ISAIAH 53:10

So often we say God won't let you out-give Him. And that's
true because God won't let you *out-God* Him, and you simply
can't outdo God. His nature is the nature of generosity. He's
generous in mercy. He's generous in forgiveness, grace, love,
and acceptance. He's not willing that any should perish, but
that all should come to repent. He is generous in every single
aspect of his nature.

The Bible says in the Book of James that everything we
have comes down upon us from the Father of lights, in

whom there is no shadow of variableness (Jas. 1:17). There's no turning. There's no changing. Everything we have that is good, God gave it to us for all time. Psalm 24:1 tells us, "The earth is the LORD's and the fullness thereof; the world, and they that dwell therein." Only God can do these things, yet the challenge remains—we are commanded to be like Him.

> And we know that all things work together for good to them that love God, to them who are the called according to his purpose. For whom he did foreknow, he also did predestinate to be conformed to the image of his Son, that he might be the firstborn among many brethren.
>
> —ROMANS 8:28–29

We are commanded to be conformed to the image of Christ, and I think one of the most nonconforming areas in the church world, at least in America, is the area of stewardship and giving. We think stewardship is boring. We think tithing is a burden. We think the same about giving and missions and benevolence and sacrifice and obedience and generosity. We've all been taught to avoid talking about money, and the reason there's so much ignorance surrounding generosity in the church is because pastors have given it a stigma, which is sadly ironic. The pastors and other church folk who say, "Don't talk about money," also say, "Just preach what Jesus preached." So let's finally do that concerning this subject.

JESUS ON GENEROSITY

Money and giving was likely the number one subject Jesus preached about. Consider this: Jesus spoke three times more often about money than He did about heaven and hell combined. He taught about financial resources so frequently because everything you have comes to you from God for reasons of His making. It's our job to obey Him whether we understand these reasons or not. I trust this book will fully demystify it all for you, so please stick with me.

God is the source of all wealth and resources, and He is the owner of it all. We are not the owners of His proverbial bank. We are the tellers. We are only His stewards, for the owner owns everything. Does that make sense? He owns it, and we are simply stewards of it.

> Moreover, it is required of stewards that they be found faithful.
> —1 CORINTHIANS 4:2, ESV

The Bible tells us we are *required* to be *faithful* stewards. Not fast, not fervent, not fancy, and definitely not frugal, just faithful. We are to be faithful with everything God has entrusted to us. So here's where the subtitle of this book comes into play. When God can trust you, He will bless you. That's the entire theme of stewardship. God is not looking for a church to bless, He's looking for a church to trust. He's not looking for a marriage to bless, He's looking for a marriage to trust. He's not looking for a business to bless, He's looking for a business to trust. Once He does find it, He will bless it. It's interesting to note that even nonbelievers can benefit from this truth.

Did you know that if an unregenerate businessman applies biblical principles to his money, his money will be blessed? Did you know that if a lost man will learn the principles of stewardship and generosity, God by His very nature will allow the law of generosity to bless that man's business, even if he's not yet himself in the fold of God's family?

Like gravity—a fixed conditional law that does not ask your permission to operate—so it is with the principle of stewardship. It is a fixed law. As we're about to explore, tithing is a fixed law, just as sowing and reaping is a fixed law. These forces don't care if you cooperate or not. They're going to work with or without your cooperation. I hope you get that. If you don't now, you will once you finish this book, as we'll dive deep into these realities as we proceed.

CHAPTER 3

OBEDIENCE GIVING: YOUR ON-RAMP TO BIBLICAL GENEROSITY

Y OU MUST FIRST understand that there are actually three types of giving: *obedience giving, sacrificial giving,* and *extravagant giving.* They're all different, and they're likely different biblically than you have been taught. We'll unpack all three as we proceed, but let's start with the primary component of obedience giving, the much maligned and terribly misunderstood principle of the tithe. It's one of the most controversial subjects in Christianity (no surprise there!), and it's more important to fully understand than most Christians realize.

You might say, "Well, Pastor, I'm already there." And I'd say, "No, you're not." I'm not. We're not. The church is not; and I'm going to prove that. None of us is truly there, and though my effort to end the controversy around the tithe is indeed one of the goals of this book, it is far from being the most important subject, so please stick with me. The truth on the matter will truly make you free.

Christendom is so ignorant about the biblical mandate of tithing that massive ministries have been built whose sole purpose is to make us feel guilty for talking about tithing. They should feel guilty and convicted for being so unbiblical and for leading so many into biblical poverty. These people are calling God's principle a bald-faced lie, and I'm calling them out. Let's disabuse them of their disobedience, shall we?

LAW OF FIRST MENTION

In Christian theology, the law of first mention is very important when studying the Bible. It says that the first time God mentions a concept, word, phrase, or pattern in the text, it establishes a foundational precedent that continues true throughout the entire Bible, from Genesis to Revelation. This may be the most important theological law there is when cross-generational interpretation comes into play, especially considering that the Bible record spans some four thousand years of world history. You've probably heard of this law—in fact, I know you have if you've been following my teaching for a while—but at the very least you realize it to be an obvious truth.

THE ORDER OF MELCHIZEDEK

For all the folks that say, "Tithing is found in the Levitical law of the Old Testament, and Romans 8 clearly says we've been redeemed from the law and are no longer under it," I say, "Yes, absolutely, but let me clarify that for you where the tithe is concerned." Abraham and Jacob (Israel), the two greatest patriarchs of the faith, both tithed to God long before the Levitical law was instituted. At the time of the *first mention* of the tithe in Genesis 14, Abraham had just won a great victory against a gang of wicked kings when he suddenly found himself receiving a visit from the most mysterious and compelling priest in the entire Bible. Hundreds of years before the Levitical law came to be, Genesis tells us that Abraham tithed to Melchizedek, king of Salem, priest of the most high God. I and most scholars believe that Melchizedek was an Old Testament Christophany—a preincarnate appearing of Jesus.

> And Melchizedek king of Salem brought forth bread and wine: and he was the priest of the most high God. And he blessed him, and said, Blessed be Abram of the most high God, possessor of heaven and earth: and blessed be the most high God, which hath delivered thine enemies into thy hand. And he gave him tithes of all.
>
> —GENESIS 14:18–20

Again, this is the first mention of the word and concept of the "tithe" in the entire Bible, and it shouldn't escape us that this tithe was made to "the most high God" through the priesthood of Melchizedek, not to the Levitical priesthood of Aaron that was still way off in the future. Even more, the New Testament Book of Hebrews tells us that Jesus is "high priest for ever after the order of Melchisedec" (Heb. 6:20), revealing that Abraham's epic first tithe transcended the law both in its time frame and its divine purpose and was ultimately made to God in Jesus. The writer of Hebrews (whom I believe to be the apostle Paul) fully explores this beautiful truth.

> We have this as a sure and steadfast anchor of the soul, a hope that enters into the inner place behind the curtain, where Jesus has gone as a forerunner on our behalf, having become a high priest forever after the order of Melchizedek. For this Melchizedek, king of Salem, priest of the Most High God, met Abraham returning from the slaughter of the kings and blessed him, and to him Abraham apportioned a tenth part of everything. He is first, by translation of his name, king of righteousness, and then he is also king of Salem, that is, king of peace. He is without father or mother or genealogy, having neither beginning of days nor end of life, but resembling the Son of God he continues a priest forever. See how great this man was to whom Abraham the patriarch gave a tenth of the spoils!
> —HEBREWS 6:19–7:4, ESV

As we read on in Hebrews, we see that even the Levites and their priestly line were in effect tithing to the priesthood of Melchizedek through their father Abraham (vv. 5–10). Right there in the New Testament, God reveals to us that the tithe is a principle that trumped the Levitical law even while it was still in effect.

The new covenant in Christ indeed overrides the Levitical law, and that includes its heavy-handed legalistic appropriation of the tithe. But we are never told that the divine practice of giving a tenth of all our gain back to "the most high God" would ever fade away. If the first mention of the tithe had actually occurred during the establishment of the Levitical law, maybe that could be argued, but it did not.

The law may have changed (v. 7:12, 18), but as the Book of Hebrews puts it, Jesus is "a priest *forever*, after the order of Melchizedek" (v. 17, ESV, emphasis added), so surely the tithe to His priesthood lives on forever. God first taught us to tithe through Abraham's encounter with Melchizedek to show us the divine purpose and blessing of the tithe. Knowing this, why would God ever put an end to it? And why would we ever want to put an end to it? Only the love of money—greed and materialism—could lead a believer to reject the blessings of the tithe. And, as you surely know, that is "the root of all evil" (1 Tim. 6:10).

JACOB'S TITHE

As if that wasn't enough, just two generations after Abraham, we saw the second mention of the tithe in the life of Jacob (Israel). When Jacob saw what we call "the Jacob's ladder dream," do you remember what he did at the end of it? He followed in his grandfather's footsteps to again prove the tithe as a divine practice for all who seek the Lord and His blessings:

> And Jacob vowed a vow, saying, If God will be with me, and will keep me in this way that I go, and will give me bread to eat, and raiment to put on, so that I come again to my father's house in peace; then shall the LORD be my God: and this stone, which I have set for a pillar, shall be God's house: and of all that thou shalt give me I will surely give the tenth unto thee.
>
> —GENESIS 28:20–22

Jacob in effect said, "Lord, You've met me here. I'm going to call this place Bethel, which means the house of God. And from this moment forward, I will give You a tenth of all that I possess because You are my Lord and my God."

Nobody told Jacob it was a law. There was not yet any form of a tabernacle or temple. There wasn't even a "tent of meeting." There was no Moses at that time. There was no ark of the covenant. There was no Decalogue—no Ten Commandments etched in two tablets of stone—and there wasn't even an inkling of the Levitical law. None of that existed yet. Do you think Jacob felt legally required to tithe? Of course not. He was simply—like Abraham before him—expressing his faith and gratitude for the promises of God, as surely this should be a timeless practice for all who pray "Lord be my God" (v. 21).

Abraham and Jacob both knew the principle of the tithe because it was a principle that was first instituted in their hearts, not on stone tablets somewhere. So the principle of the tithe was biblical truth long before it was wrapped in the Levitical law. Though we are no longer under the law, the tithe and similar principles of our faith that predate the law absolutely still apply to us. God's first commandment to "have no other gods before me" (Exod. 20:3) was also part of the Levitical law, but no one would ever suggest it no longer applies to Christians today.

Just an Option Today?

To all those who say, "OK, but I still believe the tithe is just optional today," my question is, If you are commanded to give 10 percent under the law, then why wouldn't you want to give more than that under grace? Shouldn't we want to give

30

more to the work of Jesus through the new covenant than the law required for the work of the temple through the old covenant?

With so much more to be grateful for (Jesus!), surely we should be willing to give our all if asked, so 10 percent is clearly God's starting point—not some sort of high bar of honor to aim for. Jesus teaches over and over how we should be willing to give all we have if He ever asks us, and we also know that the church would never have survived the first century if not for the saints who in fact gave all they had for the sake of the gospel. So shouldn't a born-again believer feel compelled to give more than just 10 percent? If you would be willing to give 10 percent under the law, don't you think you should want to give 20 percent or more under the grace of the gospel? That "tithing is just optional" dog only hunts when you pretend that you're generous—when you're actually greedy and love your money too much to part with it.

Tithing is without question an instituted principle direct from the heart of God that should be forever written on our hearts. When Abraham tithed to Melchizedek, was he fol-lowing a law, or did the "priest of the most high God" even ask him for it? No, because God had written the principle on his heart, just as He did on Jacob's, and mine, and on all hearts that sincerely desire the fullness of God's blessings.

Let me quickly answer a question I often hear. Many folks ask me, "Pastor Locke, do I tithe on the net or the gross?" To that I ask, "Which one do you want to be blessed over? Do you want to be 'gross blessed,' or do you want to be 'net blessed'?" Like Abraham and Jacob, you want to tithe on "all" you have gained, not just part of it. More on this subject in a bit.

God's View of Your Tithe Today

Let's take a look at this subject from God's vantage point—not mine, not the Pentecostals', not the Catholics', and not the Baptists', but God's. This view shows me how important the principle of the tithe is. Looking again to Hebrews 7, in verse 8 we see, "And here [on earth] men that die receive tithes." Of course, that's true. We humans are the ones who take up tithes and offerings, and we're all going to die. I'm a mere mortal man on the earth, and folks like me who gather and "receive" tithes are definitely going to die, but watch this. It continues with, "but there"—not here on the earth, but there in the heavenly realm—"he receiveth them."

Pray tell me why most have never studied that verse in the Bible. Keep in mind that this is in the Book of Hebrews, part of the New Covenant, and taught after the resurrection of Jesus, which reinforces the fact that the tithe is alive and well today. Likewise, it's important to realize that Hebrews specifically teaches the Jews *not* to go back under the law. Yet God said in effect, "Let me tell you something about the law." He said, "In the law, humans receive your tithes, but in the spirit, God receives them." Let that sink in. Yet still folks say, "God doesn't want our money, so I just don't think giving a tenth is important."

If God doesn't want our tithes, why would He remind us in the New Testament that He receives them, even after He removed us out from under the law? Why did He come in the form of Melchizedek to receive the tithe well before He put anyone under the law? Same answer. God Himself receives our tithes and our offerings because it's an offering unto Him, and He clearly desires this act of worship.

> Therefore let us be grateful for receiving a kingdom that
> cannot be shaken, and thus let us offer to God acceptable
> worship, with reverence and awe, for our God is a con-
> suming fire.
>
> —HEBREWS 12:28–29, ESV

YOU AND THE TITHE

While we know we are not under the burden of the 613
Levitical laws of the Old Testament, don't ever forget that
the fundamental moral principles of the Old Testament will
never pass away. We all know that, so—as noted earlier—it's
more than obvious why so many try to toss out the tithe. It's
a simple matter of greed, the love of money. I find it as no
coincidence that in the very last book of the Old Testament,
just before Jesus came on the scene in the Bible timeline, God
says:

> Will a man rob God? Yet ye have robbed me. But ye say,
> Wherein have we robbed thee? In tithes and offerings. Ye
> are cursed with a curse: for ye have robbed me, even this
> whole nation.
>
> —MALACHI 3:8–9

In Malachi 3, God is speaking to His people. Theologically,
in the Bible timeline He's referring to the nation of Israel, but
He's delivering a principle for all future generations as well.
The tithe is a gravitational law. It is something that cannot be
messed with. You simply can't change it. You can't vote it into
existence, and you can't vote it out of existence.

So watch this. In verse 8 we see, "Will a man rob God?"
Now, we look at that rhetorically and say, "Absolutely not."
But then notice what He says. "Yet ye have robbed me. But ye

say, Wherein have we robbed thee?" And he answers in two things: "In tithes and offerings."

Let me stop and inject this to further dismiss the primary argument of the money lovers who still insist that "tithing is no longer biblical because it was part of the Old Testament law, and we're no longer under the law." Do you reject offerings as unbiblical as well? Nobody reading this book would say they don't believe in offerings. Even the pagans give for the sake of those in need. So if you believe in offerings, then why don't you believe in the form of giving that precedes and *sets up* the offering? The love of money, maybe?

In Malachi God warned us about tithes and offerings in the same phrase with equal weight. Why would He ever remove one and keep the other? Can anyone give a non-laughable answer for why God would ever say the purposes of the tithe no longer matter to Him? Why would the giver of all ever dilute His emphasis on giving? He never has, and He never will. There is simply no disconnection between these two types of giving—tithes *and* offerings. The people who believe in offerings but not the tithe are deluded by fear, greed, or both.

CURSED WITH A CURSE

As we continue in Malachi, we get into the spiritual warfare aspects of giving. Namely, in verse 9, we see, "Ye are cursed with a curse." You'd be amazed how many times I've heard people say, "I'm under a spirit of poverty." If that's you, I know the first way to break it. Start tithing.

God said that if you don't give tithes and offerings, "You are cursed with a curse." When giving and generosity come up in counseling sessions, it's most often raised by married couples. Our move into deliverance ministry thinned out a lot of need for marriage counseling, as that ministry removes most of the root causes of marital strife, but in large part most couples are ignorant to this subject. I've often heard married folks say, "Our finances are just getting gobbled up. We can't get ahead. We're under a spirit of poverty. What's going on, Pastor? What are we doing wrong?" My first question is always, "Do you tithe?" And they often say, "Well, we always try to put cash in the offering bucket."

If that's you, and you often put cash in the offering, be sure to keep an accountable record of it, especially if you consider that to be part of your tithe. That may seem obvious, but you'd be amazed at how many people think the tithe is whatever they have to spare and never even consider how they're robbing God. Remember, they're not shorting the storehouse that is the local church. God says they're robbing Him. If there's anything we should want to keep good clean records of, this is it. We should do all we can to avoid being "cursed with a curse."

STINGY PASTORS?

There's a devastating epidemic in the American church, and knowing what you now know, you'll find it hard to believe: In my research over the past twenty years, I've found that more than 65 percent of *pastors* are cursed with a curse. More than 65 percent of pastors in America are robbing God!

These pastors don't even sow into the storehouse of the ministry they shepherd, so they have cursed finances, and that becomes an endless loop. They're cursed with a curse, yet they hypocritically get up and say, "Y'all better give. Y'all better fill up them buckets. Y'all better be sacrificial. Y'all better give,

give, give!" That's despicable. More than half the pastors in America don't even tithe? That's the height of hypocrisy, right there. Everything rises and falls on leadership. Nothing goes beyond the level of leadership.

You show me a church that's giving crazy amounts of money to the kingdom, and I'll show you a church whose leadership is grounded in the Bible. You show me a church that's tighter than a banjo string with their money, and I'll show you a church that is cursed with a curse.

I've noticed that the pastors who complain about the way our church gives so much money are the same ones who complain about us reading too much Bible. Our faithfulness has convicted them of their unfaithfulness. I've also noticed that the only pastors who complain about money are the ones who aren't giving any to others. I've honestly never met a faithful, generously giving and tithing pastor that fussed about money. You know why? Because they understand that it doesn't belong to them—it belongs to God—and they are faithful enough to believe His promises.

CHAPTER 4

CONSUMED WITH THE LOVE OF MONEY

THIS NEXT STATISTIC will definitely shock you. As few as 5 percent of evangelical Christians give 10 percent of their income to their local church.[1] That means 95 percent of so-called believers are robbing God and are cursed with a curse. No wonder the American church has become so demonized and anemic. No wonder Jesus said so much about money. He knew it was going to be the greatest challenge of the last-days church. He knew the church would be cursed with the curse. He knew the church would be consumed with the love of money, which is why He said:

> Lay not up for yourselves treasures upon earth, where moth and rust doth corrupt, and where thieves break through and steal: but lay up for yourselves treasures in heaven, where neither moth nor rust doth corrupt, and

where thieves do not break through nor steal: for where
your treasure is, there will your heart be also.

—JESUS (MATTHEW 6:19–21)

There could hardly be a more historically or mathematically proven Bible principle on the planet.

There's nothing wrong with having investments. I think it's
wise to have some investments if the Lord blesses and leads
you in that way. But when people get too interested with particular types of investments, they always "put their heart into
it." Let's take the stock market as an example. Folks who reg-
ularly invest there are always checking the Dow Jones and
NASDAQ. They're always checking the numbers, the deci-
mals, and the hyphens. They're always getting on their phones
to see what's up and what's down, smiling at the green graphs
and bemoaning the red ones. And they're always talking about
what's hot and what's not. Do you know why these people
are so passionate about it all? Because where your treasure is,
there will your heart be also.

Here's a bit of irony. We've been taught since our Sunday
school days that where we put our heart (what we love most)
is where we will inevitably put our money. But that's actually
backward for most people. When you put your money somewhere, your heart will automatically follow it. That reminds
me of the people who say, "If God gave me a heart for homeless people, I'd help them." I know how to remedy that. Start
giving to more homeless people, and guess what? Where your
treasure is, there will your heart be also. God gave us the
heart for hurting people. If you don't give to them, it's not
God's fault; it's just that you're putting your money where
"thieves [demons] break in and steal."

Another one may say, "Man, if I liked kids more than I

do, I'd get involved in the children's ministry." Start putting money into the children's ministry, and you'll discover God gave you the heart for them a long time ago. You've just been cursed with a curse that has numbed you to what matters most to God. Where your treasure is, there will your heart be also. Likewise, if you simply have no love for your local church or your pastor, do you know what you should do? Number one, quietly leave and start over somewhere else with a kind spirit. If that doesn't work for you, just start sowing more into your church, because where your treasure is, there will your heart be also.

This law works spiritually, and it works non-spiritually. It works in the supernatural, and it works in the natural. Wherever you put God's money, your heart will automatically follow to that destination. It's even true concerning our hobbies. I love cycling, and when I want to spoil myself, I invest in my bikes. I shine them up. I build a little shop. I can passionately tell you about the gearing and every little detail about each bike. I also name each bike, and I love to talk about how each one came into my possession. Why? Because I've invested in them, and a piece of my heart has no choice but to follow. We obviously have to keep that in check, but I trust you get my point.

All that leads to a far more important application where marriage is concerned. Husbands, do you want to fall passionately in love with your wife? Start spending more money on her. Do more for her. Invest more into her. The Bible has some wonderful things to say about spending money on your loved ones and on yourself, and we'll discuss that more later in the book. But the stingy pastors have been entrenched in the curse for so long that we've all been taught this poverty mindset in the American church, and it's time we get delivered from it. If you want to love something more deeply in your life, you just have to invest more deeply into it. Where your treasure is, there will your heart be also.

If I really wanted to know your character and your passions, I wouldn't ask for your driver's license. I wouldn't ask for your marriage certificate. I wouldn't ask for your baptismal certificate. I wouldn't ask for your ordination papers. All I'd need to see is your checking account register and your credit card statement. How a person spends God's money says more about their character than just about anything else in their life. Money is a beautiful servant but a brutal master. If you don't use it according to God's Word, it will use you to do the devil's work, and it will beat you and your family to death.

GOD'S USE OF THE TITHE

Returning to Malachi 3, be reminded that when we fail to give tithes and offerings, we are robbing from God and thereby are cursed with a curse (vv. 8–9). This curse isn't just on the individual but also on the entire nation, and of course the church in that nation. Let's now take a look at how He defines the process and purpose of this eternal pattern of giving.

> Bring ye all the tithes into the storehouse, that there may be meat in mine house, and prove me now herewith, saith the LORD of hosts, if I will not open you the windows of heaven, and pour you out a blessing, that there shall not be room enough to receive it. And I will rebuke the devourer for your sakes, and he shall not destroy the fruits of your ground; neither shall your

vine cast her fruit before the time in the field, saith the
LORD of hosts.

—MALACHI 3:10–11

Notice that a specific act is attached to the command "Bring
ye all the tithes into the storehouse." Why? So that there may
be meat in God's house. Carried over into the New Testament,
the principle here is that we take care of those who feed us
the Word of God so that they can take care of the house of
God—now and for generations to come.

Did you know the Bible says that a pastor is to be paid
for only one act? It's not mowing the grass, although we're
not above doing it. It's not stacking chairs, although we're not
above doing that either. We do these things and dozens of
other jobs, big and small, and do it all with a cheerful heart.
But a pastor of a church is ordained of God for this one job:
to labor in the Word and doctrine (1 Tim. 5:17). The apostle
Paul asked, "If we have sown unto you spiritual things, is it a
great thing if we shall reap your carnal things?" (1 Cor. 9:11).
Paul then fully explained this reality and the flow of the tithe:

> Do ye not know that they which minister about holy
> things live of the things of the temple? and they which
> wait at the altar are partakers with the altar? Even so
> hath the Lord ordained that they which preach the gospel
> should live of the gospel.
>
> —1 CORINTHIANS 9:13–14

PAY THE PASTOR

God makes it perfectly clear. They that preach the gospel
(pastors) should live of the gospel, not a side job. So they live
as "partakers with the altar" on "the things of the temple,"
which is speaking of the "storehouse" and the tithes it holds.

Do you know why the average church in America has 126 regular members? On Easter they go up to 200, 300, even 500, and then they're back down to 15, then up to 50, then 80, then back down to 40, then up to 110—you get the picture.

Tens of thousands of churches are in that bracket, and do you know why they stay in that bracket? Because the members think they are paying their pastor to do everything they themselves should be doing. For that, the pastor falls into a puppeteering trap where he has to do everything, and the church suffers because the gospel suffers.

He does all the marrying, all the burying, all the preaching, all the baptisms, all the mowing, all the painting. He fixes the roof, he fixes the windows, and he fixes the leaks. He's going to all the ball games of everybody's kids—except his own—because God forbid he miss little Johnny's ball game. Do that and the family will leave the church and go to the megachurch down the road!

Like every other healthy pastor in America, I had to get over that. I had to let go of people's unmet expectations a long time ago. If they leave over one little thing, they're not there for the right reasons. We've had people leave the church and send us a bill for the money they gave while they were here, and I've been tempted to send it back to them—but it all belongs to God, so I had to let go of that too. The only thing a pastor is paid to do is feed you with the truth of the Word of God. Until churches get ahold of that, the curse won't be lifted.

When deacon boards, elders, pastors, associate pastors, and even laypeople come to me with their money problems and say, "Our church is in a financial mess. What do you think is the first thing we ought to do?" my advice is the same even if they're broke.

I tell these folks, I don't care if it's $15, start paying the pastor something, because in doing that you will be obedient to the Word of God. Sow into the principle of 1 Corinthians 9:13–14, and God will financially bless the entire congregation.

PROVE ME, SAYS THE LORD

Returning to Malachi 3, we see God says, "And prove me." Circle that in your Bible. There's only one time in the Bible where God says to prove and test Him, and as you can see, it's all about the tithe. "Prove me now herewith, saith the LORD of hosts, if I will not open you the windows of heaven, and pour you out a blessing, that there shall not be room enough to receive it" (v. 10). That's pretty clear, right?

He's saying, do this (tithe), and I will blow your mind with blessings. Do you believe that? If you have any doubts, you are doubting your faith in the living God, which is evidence of no faith at all. We either believe God's promises or we don't believe in God. Knowing that, I find it bitterly ironic that the primary reason 95 percent of Christians don't tithe is because of their love of—and fear of parting ways with—their money. Most people live broke because they live fearfully greedy. Talk about being cursed with a curse. By choosing to live this way, they also lose out on the overflow of God's blessing.

I've never known anyone who ever honestly tested God with the tithe and lived to regret it. Instead, they eventually found themselves living in the overflow of God's blessings. Go into any church in the world and ask around. Stop people in the streets or the grocery store, in England or Africa or Thailand, and ask them if they've tested God with the tithe. You'll see that 100 percent of the time God delivered on the promise.

You will never find a single example of God failing to deliver on any of His promises, least of all the one He invites us to challenge Him on. This test is surely the first and most important crossroads on your personal journey to biblical generosity, so I pray you'll join the 5 percent in proving the Lord is always true to His Word.

FURTHER CLARIFYING THE TITHE

Before we move on from our discussion of the tithe, I want to unpack a few important facts that will help you fully grasp all we've discussed so far. First off, tithing is not really "giving." Instead, tithing is like the training wheels to true giving, which is biblical generosity.

People often claim they tithe 10 percent of their money, but it's "every now and again," and usually it's 6 percent or 8 percent or 9.2 percent, but seldom is it the full tithe and even less often is it on their gross income week in, week out. You'll hear them say, "Yeah, I tithe. I'm a big giver." As a pastor of a very large congregation, all I can say is, "Nope." To them I say, you're not a big giver, you're a beginner. Tithing is not giving or generosity.

Even I will use the term *give* when discussing the tithe, for lack of an easier word (including in this book), but for our discussion suffice it to say the tithe is not actually giving from a generosity viewpoint but instead is simply obedience to God. As we've already learned, we are commanded to tithe—not by the Levitical law but by God Himself—so, again, tithing can be seen as the training wheels for biblical generosity.

We can't talk about being extravagantly, sacrificially, and

benevolently generous until we deal with tithing, because you will never learn to be "Jesus" generous until you obediently practice the principle of the tithe. It's simply impossible.

THE FIRSTFRUITS NATURE OF THE TITHE

Nobody would discount the wisdom we find in the Book of Proverbs, so let's see what the Lord says there about the tithe. In chapter 3, He takes the tenth principle we call the tithe and uses the beautiful term *firstfruits* in its place—possibly for the people who are still uncomfortable with the word *tithe*.

> Honor the LORD with your wealth and with the firstfruits of all your produce; then your barns will be filled with plenty, and your vats will be bursting with wine.
> —PROVERBS 3:9–10, ESV

Throughout the Bible, the term *firstfruits* speaks of more than just the tithe. It always points to the "first and best" of the matter at hand. So if the tithe is supposed to be the first and best part of your wealth and income, and you're always out of money before you can consider the tithe, no wonder you're in a financial mess. Your creditors are getting your tithe. The cell phone company is getting your tithe. Your landlord is getting your tithe, and the Lord is an afterthought. The tithe is clearly commanded as your firstfruits, not your last fruits.

In 1 Corinthians 16, Paul uses the *firstfruit* term to discuss the tithe and explain the process with great clarity, further proving that the principle of the tithe was indeed obeyed by the first-century church after the resurrection of Jesus. The people of God tithed before the law, during the law, and—as we see here—also after the law.

> Now concerning the collection for the saints, as I have
> given order to the churches of Galatia, even so do ye.
> Upon the first day of the week let every one of you lay by
> him in store, as God hath prospered him, that there be
> no gatherings when I come. And when I come, whomso-
> ever ye shall approve by your letters, them will I send to
> bring your liberality unto Jerusalem.
>
> —1 Corinthians 16:1–3

God used Paul to instruct the New Testament church with
the basics of the tithe as assurance that the command and
the promised blessings are still in effect, but now with the
purity of what Abraham and Jacob enjoyed: still required, but
no longer a religious practice under the compulsion of men—
rather a transaction in the heart between the individual and
God.

Paul said in effect, upon the first day of the week, when
the church gathers together, each of you must lay aside your
firstfruit blessings of God you received that week and bring
it to the storehouse. This "first day of the week" teaching is
important to fully understand the firstfruits nature of the
tithe.

This should help us understand why the tithe should be the
first part of our increase, given before we start to distribute
our resources for offerings and our personal needs. Consider
this. If I pull out ten $1 bills right now, tell me which of the
ten bills in my hand is the actual *tithe* of that amount? It's
the one I spend first—the firstfruit—not the second, nor the
last, but the first.

CHAPTER 5

GOD'S PROTECTION PLAN

DO YOU KNOW why most Christians have their money gobbled up? Because, as we learned in Malachi 3, most Christians don't tithe, so they are "cursed by a curse" (v. 9). But for those who do tithe, God said He will "open the windows of heaven for you and pour down for you a blessing until there is no more need" and also that He will "rebuke the devourer for you, so that it will not destroy the fruits of your soil, and your vine in the field shall not fail to bear" (Mal. 3:10–11, ESV).

So to ensure no one misses this, let's break that down. God said if we will simply test Him with the tithe, He will:

- open the windows of heaven and bless us so abundantly that He meets *every* need

- rebuke (and stop) the spirit that devours our resources

Furthermore, the curse in verse 9, where a robber is "cursed with a curse," can obviously be broken once the robber obeys the law of the tithe and repents for robbing God. Who would risk being on the wrong side of this test? Evidently, 95 percent of the church and 65 percent of the pastors.

Global Vision Bible Church is a deliverance church. We battle Satan and demonic spirits and break curses every day in Jesus' name. I've written three books about spiritual warfare, and many of you reading this book may have already read them. In our ministry, we need to be a people who are well-equipped to fight the devil and his minions on every front.

I couldn't imagine throwing away the promise that God will rebuke the devourer and protect my resources from its destructive intent. This is spiritual warfare 101, and the fact that 95 percent of Christians ignore this is a horrifying reality for the church in America. No wonder it's in such a mess. It's cursed with a curse and does nothing to get delivered.

In the full reality of this message, the tithe is not just a matter of obedience and provision; it is also God's insurance policy against the devourer and the curse of the robber. And please don't miss that this "test" of God's has an opposite reaction if you fail to respond. If you don't tithe, guess what? You will not receive God's overflowing blessings of full provision, you'll have no protection against the devourer, and you'll be cursed with a curse. Take a moment to consider that.

GOD'S INSURANCE PLAN

For those of you who are thinking, "I believe all that, but I just can't tithe this week. I've got a lot of bills coming due, so I'm going to pay my bills and then catch up with God as soon as my income allows for it," your car will probably break down in less than a week, and/or there will always be some other unexpected loss or expense that keeps you in poverty. The devourer is hell-bent on devouring and destroying you financially. If you're not tithing, you're rejecting God's protection. After all, He said you're robbing from Him, so He's simply allowing you to reap what you sow. More on that later.

God will not bend His rules for you, me, or anybody else. He's not going to rebuke the devourer if you disobey Him, rob Him, and refuse His insurance plan, and He certainly won't lift the curse you willfully brought on yourself. The principle of the tithe is one of God's universal laws that you cannot change. That's why it makes stingy people mad. It's the first tenth of their income, and they just don't want to part with their money because they love it so much.

NOT SOMETHING TO BUDGET

If you believe you can't afford to tithe, I hope you see by now that you really can't afford not to. You simply can't afford to rob God. You also cannot budget tithing and expect it to make sense. Even with the tithe, we are commanded to "walk by faith, not by sight" (2 Cor. 5:7).

If you wait until you can "budget" for what should come first, as if it's less important to you than your bills and other needs and desires, you'll never tithe. Tithing will never make sense by man's wisdom. It's a matter of "the Spirit of God"—so it will never make sense when measured with human wisdom (1 Cor. 2:14). It's a matter of faith.

All of God's promises are yes and amen (2 Cor. 1:20, ESV), and you either believe that or you don't. If we walk out His commands in obedience, He will do exactly as He promised. He will meet all your needs, and He will rebuke the devourer, and you'll stop having more month than you do money. That doesn't mean there won't be times you are tested, as that's part of the process.

God will test you financially to see if you're still going to give. Giving when you have abundance doesn't require a lot of faith, but giving when you're broke is altogether different. That's when it matters most, and God will *always* honor it. Honor God with what comes first, and He will always bless you and protect your resources.

While I could share dozens of amazing stories that spring from tithing, mine included, I recently came across a few that really moved me, so I'd like to share them with you.

CONSULTING WITH A HORSE

In 1903, a man named James sold cheese from a cart in Chicago for a Buffalo, New York, cheesemaker. But he was soon released from their employment because he found himself struggling to sell the cheese. After he was fired, James took what money he had left from his original sales and bought a horse named Paddy. Then he got a small wagon and set himself up in business, selling cheese direct to customers—when he could find them.

After a very unsuccessful day, as he was putting Paddy away in his stall, James told his horse about his struggles and remarked that he needed a business partner. Being raised in a faithful Christian family, James realized he needed to recognize his priorities and set them right. As the Bible said, he needed to "seek first the kingdom of God" (Matt. 6:33), and then all he needed would be provided by his heavenly Father. So he decided on the spot, while talking to his horse Paddy, to give 25 percent to the Lord from every sale he made.

Things turned around in a very big way for a man we know by the name of James Kraft, the founder of Kraft Manufacturing Inc. That's where we get our Kraft cheese and macaroni. What turned this man's life around? Taking 25 percent of his income right off the top and giving it to God's kingdom.[1]

MOVING HEAVEN AND EARTH

R. G. LeTourneau is famous for having pioneered massive earth-moving machines that are way bigger than the ones we typically see. This man decided to give a whopping 90 percent of his income to God. He was a billionaire businessman who built an empire on 10 percent of his profits.[2] Think about that, and let it sink in. He became a billionaire on just 10 percent of his gain. How and why? It's the principle of the tithe.

Do you realize you'd be better off giving God 90 percent while living on 10 percent than you would be by living on 100 percent? R. G. LeTourneau is proof. Robbing God will never pay off, even if it may seem otherwise for a while. You simply cannot take from what rightfully belongs to Him and have your resources blessed. That's why most folks can't get ahead. When the Bible says you are under a curse, you'd better take that to heart and get delivered from it.

As we conclude our deep-dive study of the tithe and its amazing promises, please don't forget that it is not the primary subject of this book, as it's not even a matter of generosity. Remember, the tithe is obedience training—just the beginning of the journey. The tithe is the first on-ramp onto the highway of God's blessings. If that's as far as you go, especially if you do it kicking and screaming, you have kindergarten-sized faith. You're on the journey, but you're still riding with your training wheels on. How does one graduate to the next level and reap even greater rewards? I'm glad you asked.

THREE TYPES OF GIVING

As we mentioned earlier in the book, there are actually three types of giving, and the one we've already discussed—obedience giving through the principle of the tithe—is not really *giving* at all but an act of obedience to God. As previously noted, it's like obeying the fixed law of gravity, as it were. The law of the tenth is the law that commands us not to rob from God.

The fact that He rewards us for our obedience so magnanimously with blessings and protection is beautiful evidence of His own generous nature that we are called to emulate. He doesn't have to reward us for not robbing from Him. He simply loves to bless us and protect us—especially when we're obedient.

In our study of Malachi 3, we were introduced to the term *storehouse*. As noted earlier, God's storehouse today is the local New Testament church. The Bible says the local church is the "pillar and ground of the truth" (1 Tim. 3:15), and that is only true of the local church, so don't get confused by all the other types of parachurch ministry organizations that exist these days.

I'm not in any way against parachurch organizations, but there's a reason they're called parachurch. They are not the church, but they do come alongside to pair with the church. Don't miss that. Jesus didn't die for a parachurch organization. Jesus didn't die for a Bible college. Jesus didn't die for a homeless shelter. Jesus died for the *church*, and every one of those types of organizations actually should be coming out of the ministry of the local church. Their disjointed existence and mixed messaging is one of the great failures of the body of Christ.

There was a time in history when the local church *was* the nursing home. The local church *was* the hospital. The local church *was* the orphanage. The local church *was* the seminary and Bible college. The local church *was* the widow care center. And the local church was the bank to take care of each other's needs. There was a time when the local church took care of its own no matter the need, and as we learn from the Bible, that never should have changed.

So why do parachurch organizations exist? Certainly not because they're wicked and want to lure people away from the church. No, it's because of the deficiencies of the churches and the disobedient and greedy stewardship of their leaders in an increasingly demonized world. Consider the Bible colleges that used to be arms of the church.

Somewhere along the line local church leaders decided they would take the cream of the crop of their young people whom God had anointed for ministry and send them to be trained by people they didn't even know. These non-church colleges began opening their heads and filling them up with a bunch of Calvinistic nonsense and other cessation foolishness. Then they'd send them back home when they were twenty-two years old, thinking they knew more than the pastor who'd been there teaching the Bible for fifty years.

You see, there was a time when good preaching trained good preachers. The church brought up its own. But then, through bad leadership and sloth, the church began to abdicate the professorial role. It abdicated that responsibility. Again, I'm not against most non-church organizations. I'm not against Cru. I'm not against the Gideons. I'm not against the Fellowship of Christian Athletes. I contribute to each of them.

The only reason I'd ever be against them is that they're making it easier for the church to fail at fulfilling the New Testament church model we see in the Book of Acts. The local church is supposed to be the Bible distribution center. We never should have needed some other organization to fill that need. But we as the church dropped the ball, so those ministries have now had to pick it up. Thank God for them.

GIVE TO THE STOREHOUSE

What I am against is God's people going around the authority of the local church in an attempt to meet these very real needs in a way that goes against the clear teachings of the Bible. The storehouse is the local church, and that's the only place we are instructed to bring our tithes. From there, the Holy Spirit directs each local church on how to further distribute God's resources. Every other approach is out of order.

As a pastor, when I look at the stinginess in the body of Christ today and compare it to what the New Testament church did for the people of God, I say to myself, "No wonder people don't want to give to the local church!" We are not even acting like a local church anymore.

Do you know why people who have never even attended one of our live church services still give money to our church? Because we are honest and upfront about where it's all going. These folks want to give to a church that distributes God's money to other churches and other fruitful organizations, but they also want to ensure it is done biblically—through the conduit of a local church. We are greatly blessed, and our people know we're trying to give away far more than we use to operate our ministry or pay our salaries.

Since that momentous trip to Mexico at the age of eighteen, I have always been a tither and a giver through offerings, but along this journey into biblical generosity my wife, Tai, and I eventually learned how to kick off the training wheels of the tithe, broke free from playing it safe with our offerings, and truly began to give. Today we give all our book and movie royalties to the church. We also share these royalties with the missions and parachurch organizations we support, but we do all that through the storehouse that is the church.

I don't just go around town writing checks to the boys' and girls' clubs. I run it all through the church, because the power is in generosity to the kingdom we "seek first," right? And through the kingdom, we can give to other groups, other organizations, other institutions, other churches, and any non-church group as the Holy Spirit leads. But we always give through the conduit of the storehouse so we ensure we are laying up treasures in heaven, as Jesus instructed (Matt. 6:19–20).

WALKING THE TALK

For the record, regardless of what Google wants you to believe, I'm not worth $129 million. That's a laughable number. In fact, even $1 million is a laughable number. That's just ridiculous nonsense from the demonized globalists who run the media and the internet. As you know, they hate all Christian voices that call out their satanic plans and are doing all they can to remove our influence in the world, but we won't let them.

It's sad that I even have to address that, but in a book about generosity and kingdom life, I'd be failing you if I didn't share my giving testimony with full transparency. I've honestly never seen a million dollars a day in my life. I live in a modest double-wide home. I drive an eleven-year-old car. I fly economy class. I wear inexpensive clothes and giveaway watches. I could live on Ramen noodles and often do. I love them.

Our massive internet church meets in a warehouse with a tent roof, a gravel parking lot, and no internal plumbing. I have a policy that keeps me as the lowest paid man on our church's payroll, and all of our staff serves for a nominal yet sufficient wage, and we're all grateful. I'm about as no-frills a pastor as you'll ever meet, and my life has been an open book—literally!

From a net worth perspective, I know I could have become a very wealthy man by now, as the Lord has surely blessed me greatly for my giving and my obedience to Him, but it's just not in my nature to be rich in this world. I get so much joy and reward from giving generously to the needy that I've never stopped to consider my personal wealth. I'm too busy storing up treasure in heaven to think about worldly wealth, and I have zero desire to store up where moths and rust corrupt.

Likewise, when I discuss our giving testimonies or share

my own personal acts of generosity during my livestream sermons or books, it isn't intended as a boast. I would never risk violating Jesus' warning to the hypocrites who "trumpet" their giving just to "be seen" and praised by others (Matt. 6:1–4). As a public figure and internet pastor, I'm going to be seen whether I like it or not, so that's clearly not my intent.

The reason I report our generosity is to fulfill my responsibilities as the lead pastor of a large generosity-driven church that has a hundred satellite hubs around the nation and world. As the primary steward of our storehouse, I remain completely transparent with our online members, and I do that by sharing (and celebrating!) exactly how we use every dollar of God's money—as well as where we don't use it. I'm also committed to lead in that regard and ensure our global flock knows that I'm walking the same walk I exhort them to walk—that of Jesus and His extravagant generosity toward the least, wherever we go.

This is why I often testify with my stories of generosity, as I will throughout this book. That said, the vast majority of my personal giving is indeed done in secret, and the Lord has yet to temper my enthusiasm when I do testify from the pulpit. If He ever does, you can be sure I'll relent. My only intent is to please Him, regardless of the lies the liberal media and various hate groups want to spread about me and our church.

When I see pastors of multimillion-dollar megachurches building extravagant shrines to themselves while seldom if ever preaching about their personal giving or their church's generosity, it troubles me. I've got to believe it troubles their flocks as well. I think it's a big reason 95 percent of them don't tithe.

I can assure you that our church enjoys a far higher

percentage of real tithers than that, and every pastor and leader on our staff is also an obedient tither. For this I'm confident that my transparency is Holy Spirit-led. You know a man by his fruit, right?

If I *was* worth millions of dollars—like many of the stingy megachurch pastors out there are—every person in our church would know it because all their homes would be paid for by me and my wife, and we'd share with every one of them. Our people know that to be true, which is why they keep giving. We are simply trying to obey Jesus and fulfill the calling of the last-days church, as instructed in the New Testament. I believe our obedience to this call and this sort of generosity is the very reason the Lord has so blessed us and why He led me to write this book.

> And they continued steadfastly in the apostles' doctrine and fellowship, and in breaking of bread, and in prayers. And fear came upon every soul: and many wonders and signs were done by the apostles. And all that believed were together, and had all things common; and sold their possessions and goods, and parted them to all men, as every man had need. And they, continuing daily with one accord in the temple, and breaking bread from house to house, did eat their meat with gladness and singleness of heart, praising God, and having favour with all the people. And the Lord added to the church daily such as should be saved.
>
> —Acts 2:42–47

If your church doesn't operate in a way that moves the congregation to be prepared for this sort of fellowship and giving when the need arises, it isn't an obedient New Testament church. A lukewarm social club maybe, but an obedient remnant church? No way.

CHAPTER 6

SACRIFICIAL GIVING: ABOVE AND BEYOND

IF YOU'RE STILL struggling with the tithe, the other two levels really don't matter. If you struggle with obedience, the things you do sacrificially or extravagantly won't matter, as you'll be operating under a curse (Mal. 3:9). So get right with God through the tithe and the other two levels will open up beautifully for you.

Likewise, if you only go as far as the tithe through obedience, you cannot proclaim to be generous. Obedient, yes, but not generous. The Bible says, "When you have done all that you were commanded, say, 'We are unworthy servants; we have only done what was our duty'" (Luke 17:10, ESV).

So we don't get to pat ourselves on the back for doing what God clearly said we had to do and would be rewarded for doing—or cursed with poverty if we failed to do. It's one of the most commonsense, low-bar commands in the entire Bible.

> Do not neglect to do good and to share what you have,
> for such sacrifices are pleasing to God.
> —HEBREWS 13:16, ESV

Very few of us operate through sacrificial giving on a regular basis. Sure, when we see a tear-jerking missionary report, it stirs our emotions. When we see starving little kids in the videos, it always kicks us in the gut—and I'm in no way minimizing that effect. We are genuinely moved.

People often say, "I'm just going to give until it hurts." Let's be honest. I've seldom seen that. Did you know that nearly half the world—over 3 billion people—live on less than $7 a day?[1] And we think we have poverty problems in America.

When you learn to be a good steward with your tithe, God will eventually get you in a place where you can start giving sacrificially and even extravagantly. You will finally be in a position to be so blessed that He will meet every need, just as He promised, and you will want to continue pleasing Him so that you will go on to the next level of generosity. Please know that He is not against you enjoying the blessings He has placed upon you. Don't ever forget that. Once God can trust you with resources, He will bless you with greater resources. We have to break out of the mold that curses us with a poverty mindset—the poverty spirit.

When we move beyond obedience, we move into sacrificial giving and start to give above and beyond. We say, "You know what? This particular week, this particular day, this particular month, this particular offering for the year—whatever—I'm going to go above and beyond. I'm going to *sacrifice* in a way that I'll feel it a little bit."

In 2 Corinthians 8–9, which we'll discuss later in the book, we learn that we are all commanded to *sacrifice* equally, which of course points to the fact that not everyone can give equally. So we should all feel moved to say, "I want to sacrifice as much as you sacrifice." Your sacrifice may be 50 bucks, and that might be deep for you, while my sacrifice may be 250 bucks to reach equal depth. The obvious approach would be to say we should all feel called to sacrifice at an equal percentage of our wealth. A millionaire couple should give a heck of a lot more than a family of four with a median income, right?

The Bible isn't trying to get people to give equally but to sacrifice equally so that not just one family is carrying the whole load.

SACRIFICE AT THE LOCAL CHURCH

Here's one of the curses of the American church: a church with two last names—the one on the sign and the one on the biggest checkbook. When one family funds most of the church, the whole thing is run like the mafia, because the family that owns the church is the one that gives all the money. They'll inevitably find themselves operating with the "Don't make us mad or we'll take our toys and leave" attitude. When I see that dark spirit rise up, I get the "I'll call the pastor down the road and let him know you're on the way" attitude. I'm not for sale, and I don't want their blood money. If your church has one or more of those families, you'd better break that curse quickly.

If everyone in your local church would sacrifice equally, it wouldn't be just one or two families trying to carry the load for everybody else, and it wouldn't even take exorbitant amounts of giving. In this case, your church would find greater strength in the numbers of those who are both tithing and giving sacrificially at an equal level, as opposed to dumping the burden on a few wealthy families who aren't even reaching the sacrificial level and might eventually go south on you. Does that make sense?

Remember, the sacrifice doesn't even begin until you're returning your 10 percent to God out of obedience, as that's just the starting point. So for the folks that think God is interested in your compromise of a lower percentage, you're wrong. God is the One who said "You're robbing Me" if you don't return a full 10 percent.

I've heard lots of people say, "Well, I'm new at this tithing thing, so I'm going to start at 3 percent this year, and then next year I'm going to go to 5 percent, and then I'm going to go to 8 percent, and I'm sure I'll be at 10 percent sooner or later." That's like saying, "You know what? I love to rob banks, but this year I'm only going to rob five banks, while last year I robbed ten banks. And then next year I'm going to rob just two banks, and eventually I'll stop robbing altogether." Stealing is stealing, so let's avoid that backward logic.

God does not give you the option to start lower than a tenth. I tell people all the time, "Take one month, tithe on everything God gives you, and then come back to me, and if God didn't bless your socks off, I'll give you a money-back guarantee." You can't out-give Him. He challenges you to test Him on that promise, and so do I. God takes care of His children when we obey the fixed law of the tenth, and anything beyond that is your sacrifice, but you have to make sure it's truly that—a sacrifice. For some of you it's 12 percent, 18 percent, or 20 percent to make that true. When you have to actually sacrifice something other than just digits on your bank app, then you know it's a sacrifice in the sight of God.

When I started our church eighteen years ago, I told my friends I was going to give 50 percent of the church income to missionaries. They all thought I'd lost my mind. This was back in the Baptist days, and they really worked me over and talked me out of it, and I cut way back to something they agreed was "wise." So for years we struggled. A few years back, the Lord finally convicted me on this issue. He said, "I want you to go above and beyond 50 percent." From that time forward, we have committed ourselves to giving 80 percent of every dollar that comes into the storehouse. For that, no matter the storm, no matter how serious the attack from the enemy, the Lord continues blessing us. There's no other way anyone can explain how we've survived it all, and we will continue to survive because we give sacrificially.

CASE IN POINT

Please believe me when I say I can never explain how it all works in the natural. It just works. You cannot budget for what I'm about to tell you. There's no way you can white-board session this out. We are in four lawsuits with local government agencies and traffic-weary neighbors who simply do not want our extraordinarily busy and high-capacity church to continue operating on this otherwise sleepy hill on Old Lebanon Dirt Road. The media reports that it's just two lawsuits, but it's actually four because both of the lawsuits against the church also filed separately against me, just in case they can't bleed enough out of the church. They clearly believe what Google says about my net worth.

We have spent over $600,000 on lawsuits over the past two years, and it seems that, unless these people back down, we are going to be dealing with this ridiculous money drain for a little while. When I think about all the ways we could have improved the church and blessed missionaries and single moms and better funded our adoption foundation with that money, it really stings. But you know what? God keeps meeting all our needs. He always keeps the lights on.

No matter how many people wish we had burned to the ground years ago, God keeps blessing us. Why? Because we give sacrificially. Remember how our first revival started in 2019? That's why. We decided that the biggest expense every month would be our giving. We have thirty people on payroll, and you can Google it all if you'd like. None of us are getting rich—not even one—because we have a heart for sacrificial generosity. No one lives in a palatial mansion, and if they ever do, it will be because they are independently wealthy. We believe it should be impossible to get rich while working for a church. We're remnant people with a kingdom mindset—the sort of people who store treasure in heaven, not on earth—so God won't let our spiritual house fail, because He's the one who is building us.

> You yourselves like living stones are being built up as a spiritual house, to be a holy priesthood, to offer spiritual sacrifices acceptable to God through Jesus Christ.
> —1 PETER 2:5, ESV

We are far from perfect, and we've made our fair share of mistakes. Managing the unmanageable isn't always easy, but

I've learned that God will cover a multitude of mistakes if we will simply take Him at His Word concerning the tithe and sacrificial giving. If we ever tried to budget the way we give, it would never make any sense. I constantly ask, "How in the wild world did we give 80 percent of our money to other people and still keep the doors open? How was that even possible?" Only God knows.

CHAPTER 7

EXTRAVAGANT GIVING: LET IT RAIN

W E'LL SOON TAKE a deeper look into Jesus' teachings on sacrificial giving, but before we proceed, let's first discuss the highest level of generosity—extravagant giving. Anybody can be involved in obedience giving, thank God. It's the only place to start on the journey, but it's still just the start.

When you begin to graduate through your spiritual journey to reach the highest level, not only are you blessed by Him but you also get closer to Him. You receive an understanding of the Holy Spirit and the gifts and develop greater gifts. We'll soon discuss the fact that when you give, you experience a supernatural release in your life that empowers you to impact all around you for generations to come—for the sake of the gospel—and it's unmistakable.

> As for the rich in this present age, charge them not to
> be haughty, nor to set their hopes on the uncertainty of
> riches, but on God, who richly provides us with everything
> to enjoy. They are to do good, to be rich in good works, to
> be generous and ready to share, thus storing up treasure
> for themselves as a good foundation for the future, so that
> they may take hold of that which is truly life.
> —1 TIMOTHY 6:17–19, ESV

I must be entirely honest about this level. You will probably only meet a handful of people in your whole life who live
as humble, openhanded, extravagant givers. When they say,
"Hey, that guy right there will give you the shirt off his back,"
they're talking about an extravagant giver, who will probably
give you shirts for twenty other people too.

That's where I want the church to be. I want to see people
go out and live extravagantly generous lives. That's why I
often tell people in the church I pastor, "If you go to a restau-
rant and you are not a decent tipper, do not tell them you go
to Global Vision because we are a generous people, hoping to
become more extravagantly generous every year—and 'take
hold of that which is truly life.'"

INTERSECTION OF SACRIFICE
AND EXTRAVAGANCE

Whenever we eat out, Tai and I have a practice of asking the
Holy Spirit how much to tip the wait staff, and we always
let it become an exercise in biblical generosity. While I don't
necessarily consider generous tipping an example of extravagant giving (though it can be), it is at the very least a clear
way for tithers to move into the sacrificial level with greater
spontaneity in the spirit. The primary reason folks don't tip

well is because they want to keep more of their money for themselves rather than be a blessing to someone else. It really is that simple.

We all need to navigate that sacrificial crossroads along our journey, and tipping big is an easy place to start—as is spontaneously giving to a friend in need or a hurting stranger at an intersection, homeless or not. Once you get into the practice of sacrificial giving on these personal levels, it becomes far easier to get sacrificial at the church level, and you'll begin to look for opportunities to give extravagantly. Remember what Jesus said in Matthew 25: "Truly, I say to you, as you did it to one of the least of these my brothers, you did it to me" (v. 40, ESV). There could hardly be a clearer command to be generous with strangers.

JULIAN AND THE WAITRESS

I recall the first time we took Julian to dinner with us. "Jules," as I call him, is one of our associate producers at Locke Media and a young man who is wise beyond his years. I felt led to use this as a teaching moment for him, just as I have for all our own kids. The lesson has profoundly affected each of them on their own generosity journeys, so I try to continue that teaching model whenever the opportunity presents itself. Jules is now a dear friend and a generous one at that. He's also a super-clean eater, so we took him to a steakhouse where you can pick out your own steak.

When the waitress came to serve us, she apparently knew we were pastors, as she started spilling out about stuff she was going through. Her stories told me enough to know she was hurting for help, but the Holy Spirit told me even more, so I was excited about how this would affect Jules.

I asked her, "What's the biggest tip you've ever received?" She said, "Eighty-five bucks." I then asked, "What are you and your family in need of?" It turned out she lived with her parents, who were very sick, so you can imagine. I then asked, "What do you need right now?" She struggled to share that she had some school bills due, and they added up to about $500.

You must realize that is a lot of money for someone working tables and putting up with mean-spirited people who yell at her because the tea wasn't right or belittle her while complaining, "You didn't make my steak right!" (She's not even the one who cooks the steak.) Even more, you never know what your waitress is going through. She may be going through a divorce. She may have just lost a baby. But she is still out there working her fingers to the bone trying to keep her head above the misery just so you can make her feel like garbage and give her a $5 tip.

I said, "Well, ma'am, we want to bless you, so we're going to pray about what the Lord wants us to give you." When Tai confirmed what I was thinking, we knew it was God's number for her.

When I preach in other cities, I occasionally receive love offerings that give me this sort of liberty, and I had just returned from one of those meetings, so the timing was perfect. Once she saw that I gave her a $1,500 tip, the young woman threw the menu up in front of her face, fell out in the booth behind her like she was slain in the Holy Ghost, and—with a restaurant full of people wondering what the commotion was all about—screamed, "Hooh, Lord Jesus! Hoooooh!" As we walked out, I looked Jules square in the face and said,

"That's what I live for. To make people shout 'Lord Jesus!' That's what I live for."

I obviously can't always do that, but that's what made it an extravagant act for me at that moment. I have needs like everyone else, and God meets them. So when I have the means to bless someone extravagantly, I'm going to do it even if it leaves my pockets empty. As noted earlier, I'm not telling you these stories to impress you, but only to teach you. I trust that's why you're reading this book. To walk in biblical generosity, you have to believe in God's promises, and I do—every single one of them. How about you?

ONE MASTER

Giving sacrificially or extravagantly takes a dramatic shift in where you see yourself in the kingdom. If you're seeking "first the kingdom of God" as Jesus commands us, you will only store your treasure in heaven, and that requires obedience to His Word when it comes to your money. In this case, He's specifically referring to obedience to His commands on giving at all three levels.

If we try to keep our extra money for our own extravagances or "lay it up" somewhere else in this world, the money becomes our master. But if we give it to those in need as commanded, we are storing it up in heaven and proving God to be our Master (Matt. 6:24). If you're earthly minded, you may never have contemplated what it means to store "treasure in heaven," but those who are kingdom minded— heavenly minded—can't stop thinking about it. The thought of storing more treasure in heaven with God as our Master consumes us. And according to Jesus, we're all 100 percent consumed by one of two masters: God or money. You simply can't have it both ways.

> No one can serve two masters, for either he will hate the one and love the other, or he will be devoted to the one and despise the other. You cannot serve God and money.... But seek first the kingdom of God and his righteousness, and all these things will be added to you.
> —JESUS (MATTHEW 6:24, 33, ESV)

For me, money is the biggest demotivator on the planet. You ask anybody who works for me. When Wayne, our producer/ director, is leading our negotiations at Locke Media, whether it be for a film or a book deal or any of the other gospel media we produce, there's always a point where money becomes the primary topic. We've been in phone conferences and Zoom meetings with major distributors and publishers, and as soon as they start talking money to grease the wheels and win me over, he knows to shut it down. More than once I've heard him say, "Hey, can we not talk about our profit potential? We're just looking to reach the largest audience possible, and money simply will not move Pastor Locke." With a chuckle he'll add, "Really, you're about to lose him." And he's right. I never had to ask him to say that because he's been with me for a very long time, and he knows that money will never move me—only God.

MARY'S OINTMENT

In John 12 we see a very familiar example of extravagance— not obedience, not sacrifice, but extravagance. I'm not going to fully develop this passage and all it teaches us, but I do want to show you a phrase that proves this was indeed far more than just a bit of sacrifice. This was an extraordinarily extravagant act, so extravagant the Bible calls it "very costly" right there in the text. The extravagance was so over the top that it shocked everybody in the room and deeply moved Jesus.

> Then Jesus six days before the passover came to Bethany, where Lazarus was, which had been dead, whom he raised from the dead. There they made him a supper; and Martha served: but Lazarus was one of them that sat at the table with him. Then took Mary a pound of ointment of spikenard, *very costly*, and anointed the feet of Jesus, and wiped his feet with her hair: and the house was filled with the odour of the ointment. Then saith one of his disciples, Judas Iscariot, Simon's son, which should betray him, Why was not this ointment sold for three hundred pence, and given to the poor? This he said, not that he cared for the poor; but because he was a thief, and had the bag, and bare what was put therein. Then said Jesus, Let her alone: against the day of my burying hath she kept this. For the poor always ye have with you; but me ye have not always.
>
> —JOHN 12:1–8, EMPHASIS ADDED

This blessing was well beyond the 10 percent level. When we study the context to see what the Bible is really telling us here, we find that in that box was a pound of ointment with a value far beyond most anything we see today. If we were to put a price on it, it would easily be worth a full year's wages. This woman broke open a box worth a full year's salary and poured it out onto the feet of Jesus. It was *very costly*. Not many folks can say they've ever given away a full year's salary.

We may tithe, and we also may give sacrificially when the

missionary or prophet shows up. But we seldom if ever experience selfless extravagance like this. The Bible says she opened up the spikenard, anointed the feet of Jesus, and wiped His feet with her hair. The whole house was filled with the aroma of the ointment. Then Judas, the thief and betrayer, asked, "Why was this ointment not sold for three hundred pence and given to the poor?"

We see likewise that God exposes Judas' true motives. It wasn't that Judas "cared for the poor" but that he was a thief and controlled the money bag. Judas was thinking to himself, "If that had been converted to money, that would have been more money in the bag for me to steal and run off with after I turn Jesus in to the authorities." Then Jesus said, "Let her alone: Against the day of my burying has she kept this" (v. 7). We have to understand that what she did by pouring this ointment onto His feet was prophetic in nature. Jesus in effect said, "She's prophesying what's about to happen, and she's preparing Me for My burial."

Then Jesus said we would always have the poor with us. You might recall when Moses said that very same thing to the people of God (Deut. 15:11). In essence: "You're always going to have the poor around you, so you'll never be able to say there's not a need to help the poor." Both Moses and Jesus reminded us of that. "But," Jesus said, "you won't always have Me."

Here's the rebuke. Jesus was basically saying, "You do realize I'm only here for a short while longer, don't you? And you do realize you passed fifteen poor people on the way to get here just to say that, right? So why aren't you caring for them yet? You went through fifteen red lights that had somebody holding a sign pleading for help, and now you're going to fuss about the poor when you see someone do something extravagant for Me?"

For most people, giving is a matter of convenience or "show," not conviction. There's a massive difference. We see this same disparity today when some people give extravagantly with no expectations of return while others give just enough to be noticed, believing it will keep God and the preacher off their back.

Returning to our passage, Jesus said, "Leave her alone." In other words, do not try to rebuke her and absolutely do not try to stop her. In another passage, through a cross-reference of this sort of act, Jesus said:

> For in that she hath poured this ointment on my body, she did it for my burial. Verily I say unto you, Wheresoever this gospel shall be preached in the whole world, there shall also this, that this woman hath done, be told for a memorial of her.
>
> —MATTHEW 26:12–13

Did you know this is the only act Jesus ever instructed us to teach whenever and wherever the gospel is taught? I don't know how we've missed that in the church, as it should be a message we've heard without ceasing. Jesus basically said there are two things you've got to preach everywhere you go: the gospel and the power of sacrificial and extravagant generosity. A year's wages was broken over the feet of Jesus without a second's hesitation, and the only person in the story that was angered by it was a religious person—Judas, a thief and the betrayer of Jesus.

JUDAS IN OUR MIDST

Most people don't know this, but several years ago we had a man who was involved with the ministry rob us blind of everything we had. He did things with the church's money and resources that we may never learn about and eventually ran off with about $200,000. He stole all of our building fund and all of our missions money.

We had no idea he had filled his house with all sorts of ill-gotten merchandise. He even bought a boat and camper and signed the church as collateral. But because I had entrusted him during a season when we were constantly traveling, and his wife too, who had access to the books, we had no idea this was going on. He even took a church vehicle out of the church's name and put it in his own name and got liens against other assets to steal even more. He was that devious—and that trusted. I never could have imagined it and still have a hard time believing it.

This man was a stone-cold shyster, and it was a nightmare of epic proportions. After the dust settled, folks were saying, "You need to put him in jail!" And we certainly could have. We had hired a private auditor to conduct an audit, and once complete the auditor said, "I know you want to have him arrested." I said, "Absolutely I do. Absolutely." But he then informed me that because his wife was the one who cooked the books, we would also have to go after her.

> But those who desire to be rich fall into temptation, into a snare, into many senseless and harmful desires that plunge people into ruin and destruction.
>
> —1 TIMOTHY 6:9, ESV

You have to understand, I loved this man and his wife. This is why and how I came to trust him so blindly. They had prayed for years to have a baby and had finally just had one. I believe the baby was about nine months old when all this happened.

This Judas burned through $200,000 of God's money in our storehouse. I wanted to put him so far under the jail I couldn't see straight. But to do it, the baby's mama would have to go to jail too. Suddenly my heart and mind were with that innocent baby, not my need for justice against his parents. I couldn't bring myself to force that baby to grow up without parents, all over $200,000. So I didn't.

The man now lives in another state, and despite my act of extravagant kindness toward his family, today he wouldn't spit on me if I caught fire. He's become mean as a junkyard dog and bitter as all get out. He even called the news media to try to hurt me, over and over again, and I still refuse to press charges for the sake of that baby.

Here's why I'm telling you this story. As I discuss our church's extravagant generosity over the recent years, it's important for you to know that we've suffered through severe financial woes, and we haven't always had a large donor base. In fact, this crime happened just before revival broke out in 2020, so we were still a very small congregation meeting in our very small chapel. It was a crime that would end most churches. Were it not for the events that followed, it probably would have done the same to ours.

> The thief cometh not, but for to steal, and to kill, and to destroy: I am come that they might have life, and that they might have it more abundantly.
>
> —JOHN 10:10

Once I figured out the full scope of the crime, I called the elders to meet with me at my house after our Wednesday night Bible study. As we all settled in around the table, my hands were shaking as I laid out all the bank papers and other evidence before them. They asked what it was, and I said, "That right there is probably all of our resignation papers. We're done, guys." I wept. Hard.

Then Brother Mark, a good man to this day, said, "Pastor, let's just pray, and I know God will give you wisdom by this Sunday." At the time that sounded nice, but I was at a total loss for ideas. When Sunday rolled around, I just got up and shared what that man had done and confessed that we were flat broke and unable to pay any of our bills. Everybody cried.

> Bear ye one another's burdens, and so fulfil the law of Christ.
>
> —GALATIANS 6:2

Once we were all ready to dry our eyes, I got up and said, "Here's what we're going to do. We're going to take an offering, and it will literally be a start-over offering." We had already been through some very strong financial years before that, so you can imagine the feeling of failure that swept over me as I continued, "Whatever we bring in today is the only money our church has to survive."

Our small congregation consisted of maybe thirty families at the time, and they gave at a sacrificial level, but it still only added up to a few thousand dollars. I put it all in the bank the next day and determined we'd get through Wednesday service before deciding what to do with it. We had already scheduled one of our missionary families, the Wonsers, to come speak. Michael Wonser is a dear friend, and we had been supporting his family for years, so I didn't want to cancel on them.

I called Michael beforehand and told him what happened, but he agreed that God wanted him to come preach as planned. When Wednesday night arrived, I got up before the small congregation and said, "We're going to take what little bit of a love offering we can, and we're going to bless his family with it." We were already a generous people, so no one objected, but while Michael was preaching I leaned over to Tai and said, "God told me to take whatever comes in tonight and everything we brought in Sunday and just give it to him." And she said, "Well, if God said it, then just do it."

At that point I heard the Lord tell me to be as extravagant as possible. I hurried to the office when it was all over, and the ladies were in there counting what came in, so I ran over to my house to see what else I could round up. When I got back, I looked into our bank account to see what else we had left to give, and thank God, though we had just recently begun receiving from the online community, they were especially generous that night. When we got it all added up, we wrote the biggest check we had ever written for missions up till then—$7,500.

Every single dime we had was in that $7,500 check. When I handed that check to Michael, it was perhaps the most important moment in the history of our church. We've survived the un-survivable at least three times, maybe four, and the Lord did something extraordinary to resurrect us every single time.

LET IT RAIN

> One gives freely, yet grows all the richer; another with-
> holds what he should give, and only suffers want.
> Whoever brings blessing will be enriched, and one who
> waters will himself be watered.
>
> —PROVERBS 11:24–25, ESV

From the moment I handed Michael Wonser that money, God opened the windows of heaven over our church. Everyone who knows the history of Global Vision Bible Church knows that we point to that act of generosity as the true catalyst for the revival that sprang up in 2020. Because we gave extravagantly of all we had to that man of God and his family, God poured out His blessings beyond anything I could have imagined.

My stance against the Covid lockdowns was definitely an accelerant, but the revival fire had already begun. Since then we've been able to give millions of dollars to missions and needy families every year. Our social media reach and online church community exploded to a combined 4.7 million people. We've had five best-selling books and the number six faith-based film at the box office, and all this gospel media has brought incredible seed into our storehouse for the kingdom.

Have we had rough times? Of course. But we've never missed a bill, never missed payroll, and never lacked for anything since.

God said, "Son, all you had to do was practice the extravagance you preach." And that night I said, "Yes, Lord." I can look back historically at that night and know it was the night God said, "There are the people I can trust in Mount Juliet,

Tennessee, so now I will bless them." He knew all this was coming because it has been His doing all along.

HEAR WHAT HE HAS DONE!

> Come and hear, all you who fear God, and I will tell what he has done for my soul. I cried to him with my mouth, and high praise was on my tongue.
>
> —PSALM 66:16–17, ESV

When God poured out the blessings through our incredible donor base, I began keeping what I call my generosity journals. Every day of the week I write the date and the recipients of all our giving. It includes all the missionaries we support, all the babies we helped get adopted, all the widows we blessed, all the bills we paid for our members, all the churches we built, all the wells we dug, all the lights we kept on, all the people we put through addiction programs, and all the waitresses and waiters we blessed. Some days I find myself adding person after person after person, and I fill the pages from top to bottom.

Whether it's $200 or $2,000 or $200,000, every dollar of every gift blesses the givers who pour God's money back to Him through our storehouse, while storing up treasure for themselves in heaven. A very large percentage of our church family had been obedient tithers for the lifetime of our church, and we were already well known for our sacrificial giving to others. For that, God had provided for our every need through many storms. And when the devourer came to steal and destroy, the Lord rebuked him by opening up His windows of heavenly blessing.

Just a few years ago $7,500 was the largest giving check we had ever written, and it is without question an extravagant amount to give, especially when we had hit our financial rock bottom. Today we are one of the most generous churches in the world. We still don't store up treasure on this earth, because we trust that His provision will never end—as long as we remain generous toward His children. When you seek first the kingdom of God and His righteousness, God will meet all your needs, now and forever.

> O God, thou hast taught me from my youth: and hitherto have I declared thy wondrous works. Now also when I am old and greyheaded, O God, forsake me not; until I have shewed thy strength unto this generation, and thy power to every one that is to come.
>
> —PSALM 71:17–18

CHAPTER 8

RECIPROCATION: BIBLICAL MAGNETICS

WE'RE GOING TO be studying the following famous passage for quite a while in this book, and my hope is that you'll have it written on your heart by the time you finish reading the very last page.

But love ye your enemies, and do good, and lend, hoping for nothing again; and your reward shall be great, and ye shall be the children of the Highest: for he is kind unto the unthankful and to the evil. Be ye therefore merciful, as your Father also is merciful. Judge not, and ye shall not be judged: condemn not, and ye shall not be condemned: forgive, and ye shall be forgiven: give, and it shall be given unto you; good measure, pressed down, and shaken

together, and running over, shall men give into your
bosom. For with the same measure that ye mete withal it
shall be measured to you again.

—JESUS (LUKE 6:35–38)

Right off the top, notice that Jesus commands us to love our
enemies. That's not always easy, yet notice the full context as
He says, "Love your enemies and do good and lend." From
this we know that God is eventually going to put you in a
stewarding position where you will not be in lack but instead
have the resources to lend to others, even your enemies.

As He continues, we read, "hoping for nothing again; and
your reward shall be great, and ye shall be the children of
the Highest." Jesus is not saying these particular actions will
make us children of God but that they identify us as the children of God. "For he is kind unto the unthankful and to the
evil." All of us better say hallelujah to that. He is kind to us
when we are unthankful and even when we do evil. Talk
about amazing grace.

Now, watch as He sets the stage for where He is leading us
in this message: "Be ye therefore merciful, as your Father also
is merciful. Judge not, and ye shall not be judged; condemn
not, and ye shall not be condemned; forgive, and ye shall be
forgiven."

Jesus is talking about reciprocation, which operates like
biblical magnetics. Our behaviors here on earth magnetically
draw reciprocal actions in heaven. So if you want forgiveness,
you have to offer forgiveness (Matt. 6:15). Likewise, he that
hath friends must show himself friendly (Prov. 18:24).

So when you say something like "Nobody ever smiles at
me," I have to ask, How many smiles are you giving out? And

for those who say, "I just don't feel like people are very for-giving of me," I ask, How forgiving are you of other people?

If you want joy, you have to give joy. If you want friendship, you have to give friendship. If you want mercy, you have to show mercy. If you want kindness, you have to give kindness. "So whatever you wish that others would do to you, do also to them, for this is the Law and the Prophets" (Matt. 7:12, esv).

GIVE AND IT SHALL BE GIVEN

I hope you see where we are going with this. Returning to our key passage, in Luke 6:38 we see, "Give and it shall be given unto you." So here's the question: What shall be given? Answer: whatever you give. So when you give out smiles, you get back smiles. When you give out hugs, you get back hugs. By the way, this law is also true of negative actions. If you give out mean vibes, you get them back. If you give out frowns, you get them back. If you give out meanness, you get it back. If you give out being a cantankerous person, guess who you will be surrounded with? Cantankerous people. That's why it's so true when we say that misery loves company.

As a sidebar, do you know why miserable people get mad at you when you're not miserable like them? Because they want you to be as miserable as they are. Don't give in to that non-sense. Don't ever give in to the toxicity of silly unbiblical rela-tionships with miserable people, alright?

So Jesus says in effect, "Look, if you want mercy, give it. If you want friendship, give it." And then He says if you give something away, "whatever you give away shall be given unto you." But notice what He does next in verse 38. A lot of people miss this transition, so watch closely, as He is going to switch gears and start talking about biblical stewardship: "Give and

85

it shall be given unto you; good measure, pressed down, and shaken together, and running over, shall men give into your bosom."

Notice there is nothing mystical or weird about what happens when we give. It is indeed a supernatural effect, but we can clearly see that God works it in the natural through other people. Then He says, "For with the same measure that ye mete [weigh out, give out] withal it shall be measured to you again" (v. 38). In closing this command, Jesus ensured that He reinforced the magnetics of biblical reciprocity. How is that force working in your life where giving is concerned?

PACK THE SACK

When I was growing up in Mount Juliet, Tennessee, my grandfather had this massive cornfield, and I used to hate having to help him get the corn into big burlap sacks. But I have to admit I learned something back then that helped me understand what Jesus was saying.

When I dragged that huge bag of corn back up to that old red diesel truck of his, I would say, "Alright, Papaw, I got as much in this bag as I can possibly get." And he would say, "Greggy, that bag isn't even half full, Son."

He would put his hands on both sides of that burlap sack, lift his big brown work boot, and ram his foot in the top to smash it all down. He called it "packing the sack." Then he said, "Now, drag it back out there and get some more." I would drag that sack back out to the cornfield and fill it as best I could before bringing it back for him to pack the sack again. I hope you're tracking with me.

In that beautiful passage in Luke, here's what God is basically saying. If you and I participate in being good stewards of the kingdom resources He has entrusted us with, He will literally "pack the sack" more than we can handle, and far more than we could ever pack under our own power: "good measure, pressed down, and shaken together, and running over, shall men give into your bosom."

I don't know about you, but I want to live my life with a sack that's fully packed by the Lord. If by chance you're thinking, "Wait a minute; that verse is not about money," I say, you're right. It's not about money. It's about giving.

YOUR STANDARD OF LIVING

When God increases your income, He doesn't do it so you can go on a spending spree and increase your standard of living. He blesses you so you can go on a generosity spree and increase your standard of giving. Then, as you increase your standard of giving, God will in turn increase your standard of living. It's a natural process that is supernaturally powered.

At the same time, He wants you to enjoy the fruit of your labors. While completing this book, I began reading the Bible at a rate beyond anything I have ever attempted, and it has changed my life. Solomon was the wisest and richest man that ever lived, and God used him to pen the Proverbs, Song of Solomon, and Ecclesiastes in the Bible. Here's something he wrote that has convicted me.

> There is nothing better for a person than that he should eat and drink and find enjoyment in his toil. This also, I saw, is from the hand of God, for apart from him who can eat or who can have enjoyment? For to the one who pleases him God has given wisdom and knowledge and joy, but to the sinner he has given the business of

gathering and collecting, only to give to one who pleases
God. This also is vanity and a striving after wind.
—ECCLESIASTES 2:24–26, ESV

The Word is basically saying, "Do you know what God
wants you to do with the fruit of your labors? He wants you to
enjoy what you have." Think about that. The church doesn't
teach that. The church is like, "Well, you shouldn't enjoy your
car. You better not spoil your kids. You better not wear anything with a brand name." That's not what the Bible says.

From the two primary passages of Scripture we've discussed
in this chapter, we can see that if you are a good steward with
the resources God has given you—"one who pleases Him"—
and if you are faithful to give and give and give as Jesus commanded, God will give and give and give back to you. And
the more He gives back, the more you are able to give, and
He will allow your sack to be packed in such a way that you
will not only be able to give abundantly to the storehouse and
others, but you can enjoy your life as well.

God is basically saying, "Eat what you've worked for. Drink
what you've worked for. Be extravagant in some areas. Take
that vacation you wanted to take." We've placed ourselves
in bondage to the spirit of poverty for far too long, and the
impact on the body of Christ has been devastating. As we
learned earlier, the only way to break that curse is to tithe
and give to others.

NOT ABOUT YOUR WEALTH

Here's something else we all have to understand. Having
more money will never make you a better steward. That's one
of the biggest lies that's ever been told in Christianity. If you
cannot be trusted with the hundred dollars you have in your

pocket, you will never be trustworthy with a million dollars. So stop praying that you will win the lottery and have a hundred million dollars in your bank account. It's not your bank account that needs a change, it's your heart.

Have you ever watched that show called *Curse of the Lottery*? These people get crazy amounts of money from a scratch-off lottery card, and within six months to two years some of them are in jail or broke and have nothing to show for it. Here's why: a person with a poverty mindset will always go back to a broke mindset, no matter how much money you put in their hands. It's a generational curse. They don't need more money; they need biblical management of the money they have.

We may both live in the Nashville area, but I'm Greg Locke, not Dave Ramsey. I'm not telling you to cut up your credit cards or enroll in a class on how to balance your books. I'm also not talking about good debt versus bad debt, buying a house, making investments, or buying stocks and bonds. Of course I believe in giving. And of course I believe in saving. The Bible even says that a wise steward will leave an inheritance to his children's children, so that clearly requires building up some wealth (Prov. 13:22). Knowing all that, we need to realize that whatever we are not planning to leave to our heirs, we need to use now. Spend it. Bless the people around you. Bless yourself. Bless your family.

Have you ever seen the movie about Scrooge, titled *A Christmas Carol*? What a miserable human being. I know a lot of Christians in America who are just like him. They have to have more, more, more. They've done nothing with what they already have, so why do they want more? It's greed—the love of money.

Solomon wrote, "The sleep of a laboring man is sweet, whether he eat little or much: but the abundance of the rich will not suffer him to sleep" (Eccles. 5:12). In other words, the more you have, the less sleep you get. The more you have, the more you have to worry about and keep track of, and the more intricately detailed your management mind has to be. Having more will not make you a better steward, and becoming a better steward does not begin when you finally have more. Better stewardship begins right where you are now.

You Have Enough

Too many people have a mindset where they're constantly praying, "Lord, please give me more so I can give more." But God will never give you more if you can't handle what you already have, because what you already have is already enough. As we'll soon see, Jesus commended the widow who gave her last two nickels, so we know we all have enough to give back to God (Mark 12:41–44).

If you say, "I have nothing," you'd better give your nothing away while you still have the chance to give it. God, in turn, will give you something in return. Give God something to work with, and He will work with you. I'll say it again: what you have is always enough to give. Look throughout the Bible for evidence—God loves to call the people who have little to nothing and use them to change the world. Maybe you're next.

Here's an example: in the Book of Exodus God came to this stuttering prophet of a man named Moses. It's interesting to note that forty years earlier, Moses never stuttered and never missed a beat. The Bible says he was one of the most learned people in Egypt, and as a member of the royal court he had everything he could ask for. But God put him in the wilderness on the backside of the desert in a cave for forty years and taught him how to be a shepherd. You see, God didn't need Egyptian education or great wealth to lead His people to the Promised Land. Through Moses we learn that God will beat Egypt out of you to put heaven in you.

To paraphrase, God told Moses, "I'm about to send you to Pharaoh." And Moses said, "Who in the world am I that Pharaoh is going to listen to me when I say, 'Let my people go, for the Lord has sent me?' This man has ten thousand gods that he considers lord. He is not going to listen to me." God responded, "Hey, Moses, what's that in your hand?" Moses didn't say he had a winning scratch-off lottery ticket, keys to a Porsche, or a check for a million bucks. You know what he said? "A stick." And God said, "OK. That's enough. Let's go to Egypt and change the world."

What you have is enough. Moses didn't need anything but a stick for God to use him to whip Egypt, because it was never about the stick but the God who provided the stick. What you have right now is enough, no matter how small. I know you might be saying, "That's fine in theory, but that just doesn't make sense on paper." You need to stop trying to put the principle of supernatural stewardship on a piece of natural notebook paper. It will never work. If you don't get God's perspective and take God out of the box, you will never get it—and you will never give.

Remember how I started my generosity journey? I was eighteen years old and didn't even have a job. It doesn't matter where you are or what you have. It always starts right where you are. Whether it's fifty bucks, five hundred bucks, five thousand bucks, or fifty-five thousand bucks, whatever it looks like for you, God wants you to know that what you have is enough. If you don't start where you're at right now, you will never get where God wants you to go. Please take that to heart. Don't forget that Jesus said, "Good measure, pressed down, shaken together, and running over, shall men give into your bosom." If you will obey the economic principles of God's kingdom, God will bring you resources through other people in the most amazing ways.

YOU CAN'T OUT-GIVE GOD

At the onset of this journey I set myself on a mission to prove that you can't out-give the Lord. The problem is, everybody in the church says it, but very few have ever tried it. When God opened the windows of heaven for us after emptying our bank account with that $7,500 missions check, God took my mission—my generosity journey—to the next level. If emptying our bank account through a benevolent act sparked revival at our church, I decided to see if I could just give myself right into the poorhouse, metaphorically speaking.

Individually and in my leadership role at our church, I have tried to see if I could out-give God—fully knowing that it's impossible. I say, "Lord, let's just give it all away." We've had many stories in the years since that make that $7,500 check pale in comparison. And with every check written, God just keeps on giving it back as unexpected money comes in from unexpected places. It just does.

When we first got into this large tent we currently meet in, we abstained from taking a single dollar from the weekly offering for the entire month of January, and we didn't take up a Sunday offering or a Wednesday night offering for our church needs. Instead, we let the church know we were going to give every dollar away to missions and other folks in need. We still made payroll. Still paid the bills. Still managed the lawsuits. I've decided, no matter what happens, I am going to take God at His Word and continue to prove the Bible is true in the area of giving. He will not let you out-give Him because He will not let you out-God Him.

I'll admit, all this giving is fun. It's a joy to live your life in a way that empties yourself out for the sake of others. Of course, I let the Holy Spirit lead me through it all, and I can't help everyone, but I'll never stop trying. I used to have a little sign that said, "Live simply so that others may simply live." Isn't that good?

LENDING TO THE LORD

He that hath pity upon the poor lendeth unto the LORD;
and that which he hath given will he pay him again.

—PROVERBS 19:17

A lot of people have next to nothing for a lot of different reasons. The Bible has much to say about supporting those we call the unhoused, the poor, and the homeless. As we see from Proverbs 19, it also says that when you give to the poor, you lend to the Lord. Have you ever thought about that fact? When we lend money to God in this way, we literally get it back and more. We'll talk a lot about that as we move through this book.

From Genesis to Revelation, you will never find a single person who was magnificently and miraculously used by God while being stingy. Again, I'm all for stewardship of our resources and for saving a proper amount. I believe in the Joseph principle, where we lay some aside when a famine is coming (Genesis 47). But far too often stingy people hide behind the flimsy excuse of frugality. I hear, "Well, I don't give a lot because I'm just being frugal." To that I say, no, in reality you don't give a lot because you're stingy.

There's no such thing as frugality in the Bible. Yes, we lay aside. Yes, we stay prepared for what is to come. And yes, we have oil in our lamps and also in our jars (Matthew 25). But at the end of the day, you have to do your giving while you're living so you know where it's going. God will take care of the details.

Some folks say, "I'm going to will all my money to the church to make sure they get all my money when I'm dead." Did you know there's not one single verse in the Bible that tells us God will bless us on money we give after we're dead? That said, I thank God for people who leave money in their wills to Christian organizations. Just a few months ago we received a check for $50,000 from a deceased man in Lebanon, Tennessee, that I'd never met a day in my life. I wouldn't know who he was if I saw a picture of him.

The letter from his lawyer said he had been secretly watching my sermons for years. Of course, I'm grateful for the blessing, but I wish this man had given it to us while he was still alive, as that would have produced even greater blessings for him and the church. Besides, I also wish I had the chance to thank him and celebrate his giving with him. I truly believe God wants folks to give while they're still alive, as it means so much more when they have some skin in the game. We have to recognize that all God has given us *now* is for that—it's for *now*.

CHAPTER 9

THE LAW OF POSSESSION

IN THE NEXT three chapters I'm going to give you three principles of biblical generosity (giving), but let's be clear: they are actually fixed laws. God's principles and instructions are never mere suggestions, but commands. You can argue about a law, but it is still a law. You may get some grace when you argue about the validity of a law, but it's still a law that cannot be changed regardless of your argument.

The law on Old Lebanon Dirt Road—the road where our church is located—demands a much slower driving speed than I like. But it is still the law. So when "the law" pulls me over for speeding, I can say, "Hey, man, I was in a hurry. I have to preach. I'm here to do a wedding. I'm here to do a funeral." But the law is still the law. If I don't obey it, I will regret it.

Our unwillingness to obey God's Word to the letter is

the core problem in the lukewarm, last-days church. In the apocalyptic portion of His Olivet Discourse, Jesus warned us, "And because lawlessness will be increased, the love of many will grow cold" (Matt. 24:12, ESV). You do not want to be found lukewarm when Jesus returns. If you want to live without regrets, get right about the law of God and about love, as they are interconnected.

As we look back at our key passage on giving in Luke 6, we see that Jesus is teaching us three undeniable laws. Principle one is the law of possession. This law teaches us that we own nothing and are only the stewards of everything we have because God gave it all and owns it all. We are nothing more than the tellers at His bank. We work for the president, who is in the office above us, but we do not own the vault. We only have keyed access to the vault, and the keyed access is taken away if we don't respect the vault.

Now let's take this law into account as we reflect on the tithe. God doesn't ask for the 10 percent as if that's the only portion He owns. He owns the remaining 90 percent as well. God owns all of it. That is the law of possession. I am not the owner; I am an overseer. The test He offers in Malachi 3 is a reciprocating test. That's clear in the text. To be an effective overseer, we must trust Him to provide, but we must also show ourselves to be 100 percent trustworthy with His provision.

I am not the owner of the bank. I am an overseer of the money in it.

If you are not a faithful overseer, the Bible says you will never be counted worthy to be a bigger overseer, because to whom much is given, much shall be required. If we are

The Law of Possession

faithful in the little jots and tittles of life in Christ, we will be faithful in the larger areas of life as well.

To God, Time Is Not Money

People like to say that stewardship is not just about money. They say things like, "Well, I'm tithing my *time* to the Lord." That's all good, and I get their point. But there is not one single verse in the Bible that says you can tithe your time. Tithing is strictly about money. Tithing is about possessions. Tithing is about mammon (money and possessions). Tithing is about firstfruits. With the tithe, God is trying to help us crucify our flesh regarding the love of money, not the love of time.

A dear friend in our ministry has a massive heart for volunteer service, and for more than a decade before coming to Global Vision, he served tirelessly in the ministry every week, for no compensation. It added up to well more than 10 percent of his time. He came out of a ministry that erroneously taught that this time investment constituted his tithe, because—after all—time is money, right? Wrong. Time can never be a firstfruit. It also can't be tithed. Despite this brother's very fruitful service to God, he could never really get ahead, as the devourer always seemed to undermine and steal away his best business ideas and investments.

He has told me some of the financial horror stories he endured while under the curse of that bad teaching, and his losses were often staggering. He continued to trust and serve while working to crucify his flesh in all other areas, but no matter how "right" he got with God, the devourer still had an open door through his disobedience with the tithe. He was cursed with a curse.

When he began serving at our local, he came to me for counseling over this issue. Once I set him straight, he eagerly began tithing and giving more generously—no longer just with his time, but now also with his money. Four years later, he has never been more blessed with his finances, his business efforts have a clear anointing on them, and even his service ministries have become more fruitful, well beyond anything he experienced before the tithe.

I know dozens of stories like this, so please take it to heart. If you're a faithful servant in the ministry but simply can't get things to come together for you, get right with God concerning generosity and selflessness with your resources, starting with the tithe.

Your service to God is required, but it will never be counted toward the tithe. It's no wonder why pastors don't talk about this subject on Sunday morning with the livestream cameras going. Folks hate to hear the subject raised, and most are simply under the curse of bad teaching, so they're all cursed with a curse. That's why I'm compelled to teach about the tithe and biblical generosity. I am not under any such curse, and it's my responsibility as a shepherd to ensure you aren't either.

Returning to principle one, if you are not a faithful steward, it's because you don't understand who owns what you have. My shoes are owned by God. That's why I can easily give them away to someone who needs them more than me. I wear Invicta brand watches. Not Rolexes. I love Invictas and have a bunch of them because I like to give them away to men who could really use a watch.

Whenever I give one away, within a week I'll get an Invicta watch in the mail. In fact, now that I'm writing this, I expect somebody from DHL will eventually bring me a whole tray of Invicta watches. Or I will get another letter from a lawyer saying, "You're not going to believe this, but the man who makes Invicta watches died and has been watching you secretly and gave you the whole company." I say that in jest, but I trust you get my point.

Because I have been living under the blessings of sacrificial and extravagant giving for so long, I can't give stuff away fast enough.

JUST GIVE IT AWAY

I had a pair of white Nike tennis shoes that suddenly disappeared on me, and out of reflex I blamed my son Evan, because he's always borrowing my stuff, and I let him. So I said, "Evan, you took my Nikes, didn't you, Son? I know you did. Where're my Nikes?" And of course he said, "I don't know, Dad." So I said, "Go check your trunk, Son. You've got my Nikes, I know it. Where did you hide them? Did you give them to your friends?" I just couldn't find them, and neither could he. My white Nikes were gone, and I really liked them, so when they disappeared like that, the whole family knew I was bummed about it.

A couple of weeks later my wife, Tai, bought me a new pair, but she accidentally got a half-size too big. It was not so bad that I'd complain. I didn't mind flopping around a little bit like Bozo, and I don't think anyone noticed. That next Sunday I wore them to preach when, prophetically, the Lord began to talk to me about the guest pianist who was filling in that day, and I felt led to give him those brand-new oversized white Nikes. So I took them off and gave them to him right there on the spot.

From there I walked out of the tent with just my socks on (I kid you not), went directly to my house, which is on the campus, and put on another pair of shoes then came back to lead the baptisms at the end of the service. While I was baptizing folks, Tai was already at the house getting lunch ready for me and the kids and whoever else was coming over.

When I wrapped up the final baptism and finally got home, Tai said, "Honey, you are not going to believe this. I was in the closet putting up a few things, and I dropped something that rolled under that lower shelf in there. When I got down on my knees to look for it, lo and behold, I found those shoes you thought Evan stole."

Do you see what I'm saying? I can't even give my shoes away without God giving them back. Because I operate deeply in the law of possession—that God owns all of it—it's easy to give it away. Knowing He will give it right back makes it even easier.

SHAKEN TOGETHER AND RUNNING OVER

I recently gave away my Bubba truck, which was featured in our movie, and some folks were surprised I would do that. I've given three of my racing bicycles away, and I liked them way more than I liked my truck, so giving away that truck was not that big of a deal to me. When someone asked me how I would get around without my truck, I said I'd use my wife's vehicle when needed or else I'd walk or bike there. I happily did that for about three weeks until somebody basically gave me his used (but very nice) BMW.

The guy goes to our church, so he approached me and offered to sell me the BMW for what he owed on it, which wasn't much. Then out of nowhere somebody called me and gave me the money to buy the BMW. I thought, "My goodness, this is crazy. I'm living in upgrade mode all the time."

Now, I know what you're thinking: "Sure, that might happen to an internet pastor like you, but what about me?" The point is, the principles and laws of giving are the same for all of us, even if the scale might be different. Make note that I never entered any of these giving situations expecting anything back, and I was always ready to enjoy whatever came next, even if it meant walking around town or walking home without shoes on.

Once you start obeying God with your tithe and your giving, in humility and patience with the right spirit, He will indeed return it and bless you, often with interest, here in the natural and in heaven—"good measure, pressed down, and shaken together, and running over" (Luke 6:38). This is where we find giving principle two, God's law of promise, which we'll dig into in a bit. Until you truly test Him in this regard, you have no right to doubt it, so just do it and see.

You simply can't out-give God. And if you know anything about me, you know that was a huge step for me to even take that sort of vehicle. I've had this mindset for years where I was concerned about perception. I'd think, "Oh, my goodness! What will my haters say if they see me driving a BMW? They might start believing that nonsense on Google." Yep. They might also believe that nonsense if I walk barefoot or ride around town on a Huffy bike. The haters will believe nonsense about me and you no matter what we do. So why let it matter?

We need to enjoy the blessings that God gives us (Eccles. 2:24–26) and just keep giving to bless everybody else. The law of possession teaches us that our house belongs to God, our vehicles belong to God, our clothes belong to God, and—guess what?—our children belong to God. We are stewards of our children. We are also stewards of our trials and temptations. The point is, every area of our life needs to operate with an understanding of the law of possession. God owns it all.

GIVING STUFF WE DON'T OWN

When I think about it, I would have no problem giving your car away if you asked me to do it. But I might have to pray a little longer to give mine away. I could even give your house away, and I could easily give your watch away. None of that would be a big deal to me. Why? Because the law of possession tells us that once we realize we are commanded to do it, it's way easier to give away something that belongs to someone else than it is to give away something that belongs to us. This is why it's crucial to realize none of it belongs to you.

Here's what we have to understand. It should be equally easy for all of us to give away God's resources. He's the one who places His resources in our hands and instructs us in turn to give generously. So it should be easy to give it all away, especially since He promises more where that came from. It's not your house; it's God's house. It's not your stuff; it's God's stuff. It all belongs to God.

Honestly, if you really want more stuff, you have to quit stuffing the stuff and start giving the stuff away. Did you know that one of the fastest-growing multibillion-dollar industries on the planet is the storage unit industry? We humans like to stuff "stuff" that we don't need. The problem is not that we have stuff and money (mammon); the problem is when the stuff and mammon have us.

When you trust God as the owner of it all, He will both replace it here in the natural and add it to your account in heaven, which is eternally more important. When you're kingdom minded—heavenly minded—that will always make sense. I hope you're getting that. As we transition to discuss the next principle, let's take another look at Jesus' most piercing words on this matter found in Matthew 6, but this time from the King James:

> Give, and it shall be given unto you; good measure, pressed down, and shaken together, and running over, shall men give into your bosom. For with the same measure that ye mete withal it shall be measured to you again.
>
> —JESUS (LUKE 6:38)

That leads us into the second principle of biblical generosity, which is the subject of our next chapter.

CHAPTER 10

THE LAW OF PROMISE

A s we return to our key passage in Luke 6, we find our second giving principle: the law of promise. This law tells us that whatever we give, God will give it right back. Kindness comes back, money comes back, friendship comes back, smiles and hugs come back, meanness comes back, anger comes back. Everything good, bad, or indifferent comes back to you. In Proverbs we see that a soft answer turns away wrath (Prov. 15:1). Here we see the same basic principle at work.

Give, and whatever you give *shall be* given back. When God says something *shall be*, He's saying, "This is an absolute, uncompromising fact." You give, and whatever you give *shall be* given back.

Where the law of possession says that God owns it all, the law of promise says if you give what God owns, He will give it back to you. We obviously don't give in order to receive, but we all have to learn to receive in the right spirit. Why is it we believe every promise in the Bible but that one? We believe whosoever shall call upon the name of the Lord *shall be* saved, right? You believe it so much that you know for a fact you are going to heaven, because you repented and asked Jesus to forgive your sins, right? If you can believe that unmatchable promise, why can't you believe this one?

If we can believe that demons still tremble at the name of Jesus, if we can believe that cancer still flees at the name of Jesus, and if we can believe in the supernatural unleashing of the gifts in the life of a believer, then why can't we believe "give, and it *shall be* given"?

The law of promise in giving is effectively the biblical law of sowing and reaping. What you sow you reap. Don't forget that lost people and saved people both live under the same laws. That's why I earlier said that a lost, unregenerate, non-churchgoing, Bible-denying businessman can institute biblical principles of generosity and see his business blessed. The law of promise operates for everyone on the earth.

When a believer gives with intention while understanding God owns it, then it *shall* be given back. That's the promise. It's fixed. You can't change that. If you give out watches, you get back watches. You give out love, you get love. The most loving people I know are the ones who receive the most love. The most encouraged people I know are the ones who are giving out the most encouragement. Give, and it shall be given. It's the law of promise—the law of sowing and reaping.

THE ONE WHO TEACHES

I think the reason this law has been so incredibly misunderstood in the church is because it's seldom taught in the church. No one likes to talk about seed because no one likes to talk about sowing. For that, the church is in a serious pickle. We are in a financial mess because we don't want to talk about the giving principles of God. Yet God says:

> Let him that is taught in the word communicate unto him that teacheth in all good things.
> —GALATIANS 6:6

The King James word *communicate*, in this context, has a very specific meaning that might help explain why so many churches are struggling today. Let's see how the ESV translates that into our modern English:

> Let the one who is taught the word share all good things with the one who teaches.
> —GALATIANS 6:6

As you can see, *communicate* in the King James means *share* or *give*. In our study of the Bible, we have to remember that every verse has multiple applications, but it will only have one theological interpretation. There's only one way you can interpret a particular verse, but there are multiple ways to apply the verse. So we see in Galatians 6:6, the apostle Paul wrote, "Let him that is taught in the word share all good things with the one who teaches." Let me remind you that the epistles, books like Galatians, Ephesians, Philippians, Colossians, and 1 and 2 Corinthians, were all written as letters to the local church they're named for, so Paul was teaching as a pastor in a local church context while he was still living out the stories we read about in the Book of Acts.

At first glance the scripture we just read might seem self-serving, but what Paul is saying is the person who teaches the Word of God to you should be financially blessed by you for one reason—they are teaching the Word of God to you. That's what the Bible says. He that preaches the gospel should live of the gospel.

When we touched on this subject earlier, it was from the perspective of the tithe, but in this passage (Gal. 6:6) God is pointing directly to the law of sowing and reaping, so let's revisit it here.

It may surprise you to learn that a very large percentage of lead pastors at small churches are part-time employees of the church, and many are volunteers. Why? Because they believe they can't afford it. But if churches in America were stewarding resources properly, I believe every church would have a full-time pastor. One of the reasons these churches have budget problems is because a part-time pastor produces a part-time ministry.

I'm not saying they should make the guy rich or pay him extravagantly. I'm saying that when somebody teaches the Word, the church should communicate with their pocketbook, not just their mouth. You can't grow your church with lip service.

That's basically what Paul is saying in 2 Corinthians 8 and 9, as we discussed earlier. With Galatians 6:6, he brings it together and says in effect, "If I have sown into the spiritual things, it's not a big deal that you sow back to me through your carnal things, your mammon." Remember, money and stuff are not evil. It's the love of them that is evil. It was God who established the system in the local church, so that's the only way it should be done.

Now that Paul has turned on the ignition of giving, he's going to mash the gas and talk about giving in a context we never heard before. After writing, "Let him that is taught in the word communicate unto him that teacheth in all good things," Paul immediately tells us why that is a command of God:

> Be not deceived; God is not mocked: for whatsoever a
> man soweth, that shall he also reap.
>
> —GALATIANS 6:7

As noted earlier, the law of sowing and reaping is a universal law in the application of all things. But in this passage he is speaking of this law in the context of a single interpretation, and it's all about the use of our money and resources. He is talking about communicating (sharing) all good things financially with those that teach us the Word, and he is indeed going to broaden the scope of the context as he continues in Galatians, but don't miss what he is warning in relation to our giving. He says don't be deceived when it comes to giving money: "God is not mocked: for whatsoever a man soweth, that shall he also reap." Now look what Paul writes in the very next verse:

> For he that soweth to his flesh shall of the flesh reap cor-
> ruption; but he that soweth to the Spirit shall of the Spirit
> reap life everlasting.
>
> —GALATIANS 6:8

Once again, he is not saying that having these things is evil. In verse 6 he even called them "good things," so the resources are not the problem. Paul is reinforcing what Jesus said in

Matthew 6. Here's the unified message: If you like to buy clothes and bikes and cars, that's great, but you must know that your stuff will eventually wear out, as moth and rust will corrupt it all, or thieves will eventually break in and steal it. If you spend all your God-given resources on stuff, that stuff can be made into a bucket of bolts at the next stoplight down the street. If you sow to your flesh (your carnal desires), you'll just reap corruption.

Of course, this law also applies to pornography, adultery, and other sins of the flesh, but don't miss the context of this passage, as He is only talking about money in this specific verse. So let's read that again. "Be not deceived; God is not mocked: for whatsoever a man soweth, that shall he also reap. For he that soweth to his flesh shall of the flesh reap corruption; but he that soweth to the Spirit"—that is, heavenly things—"shall of the Spirit reap life everlasting." It's one way or the other. Through all the sowing of your resources, you're either reaping corruption or you're reaping "life everlasting." I can tell you this much: you don't want to be on the wrong side of that. God will not be mocked.

When God promises that we will reap "life everlasting," He's referring to the things that last, the things that are eternal, the things in heaven, where moth and rust do not corrupt and where thieves do not break through and steal. "For where your treasure is, there will your heart be also" (Matt. 6:21). If you need more evidence that Paul is still writing about the use of our resources, look at the very next verse he wrote in Galatians 6:

> And let us not be weary in well doing: for in due season
> we shall reap, if we faint not.
>
> —GALATIANS 6:9

That verse is often misapplied and taken out of context. When Paul writes, "Let us not be weary in well doing," he is directly referring to what he writes in the next verse. He's talking about our stewardship, our giving of the resources we are commanded to sow into the kingdom. So don't grow weary in well doing, for in due season you shall reap—if you faint not. When? In due season, if you don't faint.

We've been taught to tithe on Sunday and be blessed on Monday. But that's not what God says. He says we'll be blessed "in due season." The church is consumed with "you season," but the Bible is consumed with "due season." It's not about you, nor is it about instant gratification. You may not be due yet, so don't grow weary, and do not faint.

So what does Paul mean by that? Simply this: do what God said knowing that God will turn things around. Don't give up on God. I've watched churches, individuals, marriages, and whole businesses give their way out of massive debt. I've seen it happen in our church too many times to count. Why? Because if you faint not, the due season of reaping shall come upon you—sometimes when you least expect it. This brings us to verse 10, where Paul writes:

> As we have therefore opportunity, let us do good unto
> all men, especially unto them who are of the household
> of faith.
>
> —GALATIANS 6:10

This is the kicker. How do we do good? By our giving, and not just to the people we hear preaching and teaching. "Let us do good unto all men, especially..." Make note of that qualifying word *especially*: "unto them who are of the household of faith." Do we bless all sorts of people around us? Absolutely.

But the main people we focus on blessing are the people of God, and the "doing good" opportunity is empowered by the principle of sowing and reaping. Give as instructed, and it shall be given unto you as promised.

THREE LAWS OF SOWING AND REAPING

Here's the law of sowing and reaping in a nutshell, and it's very straightforward. This principle is actually comprised of three simple laws that will make it easy to remember and apply. Law one is about the *what* of the matter:

1. You always reap *what* you sow.

When you put corn in the ground, you don't get tobacco. You get corn. When you put beans in the ground, you don't get tomatoes. You get beans. When you put a certain tree in the ground, you don't get fifty other types of trees. You only get that certain tree. You always reap what you sow. Why? Because forgive and it shall be forgiven. Give and it shall be given. Whatever you mete out will be meted and measured back to you again. So you always reap what you sow.

Law two:

2. You always reap *more than* you sow.

If law two wasn't true, then farming would be nonexistent because nobody would waste their time. Why would you put a kernel of corn in the ground only to reap a kernel of corn from the ground? Who would waste such extravagant amounts of time to do that? Nobody. Not only do you always reap what you sow, but you will always reap more than you sow. If you can put one kernel in the ground and get a stalk containing thousands of kernels, what would happen if you planted thousands in the ground? You would produce literal millions.

God doesn't just add, He multiplies. In Acts 2:47, we read, "And the Lord *added* to the church daily such as should be saved" (emphasis added). Did you know that's the only time the Bible ever says God *added* to the church? Do you know what word He uses after that? *Multiplied.* As the church grew, as the men and women of God sowed and reaped for the sake of the gospel, God went from addition to multiplication. Why? Because supernatural kingdom economics works on a higher level than natural human economics. And that brings us to law number three:

3. You will never reap *anything* until you sow.

That's the law of sowing and reaping. You always reap what you sow. You always reap more than you sow. But you will never reap anything until you sow. Some people say, "Well, I don't have a lot to give, and what I do have I need." If you want to see God open the windows of heaven in your finances, you'd better give it away while you have it, because God's not interested in how much you have. He knows how much you have. God's interested in your heart and where you have it.

CAST YOUR BREAD UPON THE WATERS

You don't have to have a lot to be a generous giver. Simply give what you do have, and God promises to give it back with interest. Give God something to work with. Sow it in the ground of the kingdom while you can. You may say, "I'm down to my last twenty." Well, you'd better find somebody to bless with that last twenty. Give the sun something to shine on. Give the rain something to rain on. Give the wind something to blow on. Give God something to bless.

> Cast your bread upon the waters, for you will find it after
> many days.
>
> —ECCLESIASTES 11:1, ESV

When we picture casting bread upon the water, I think, "What in the world? That would be a soggy mess in no time." But in actuality the word is referring to the grain that produces the bread. Theologically, there are a couple of double-edged-sword contexts to the meaning of that verse, but for our application it's a reference to the principle of sowing and reaping.

Have you ever dropped something in the ocean along the shore? Do you know what it eventually does, no matter how long it takes? It always comes back, because the tide always brings it back in. And God basically says, "Put your seed on the water, and it will eventually come back to you. Don't grow weary and don't faint; just wait on Me, and I will bless your socks off."

In regard to one of the double-edged-sword interpretations of that verse, we can also apply it this way: Why would anybody want to cast upon the water something they are supposed to eat? Why would you waste what you have on something that's going to gobble up your resources? It seems like a waste, but what God is saying is, even when it seems like your giving is not making a difference, just keep doing it and watch what eventually happens. The more you do it, the more you will understand mathematically that it really does work even though you can't explain it. In truth, you don't need to be able to explain it. The law works even when we don't understand. We just need to obey.

There are certain things about God I can't explain, nor do I want to. Deuteronomy 29:29 says, "The secret things belong unto the LORD." I've had people say, "Hey, Brother Locke, I read that verse about the secret things of God. What do you think the secrets are?" And I say, "I don't know. They're secret." There are some secrets that God is never going to share with us. And I believe the workings of kingdom economics are among those secrets.

I've heard atheists say, "I want you to explain the bigness of God." If my three-pound brain can understand and explain to you the bigness of God, I'm looking at the wrong god—a god so small he's not worthy of my worship. God is far too great—too omnipresent, too omnipotent, and too omniscient—for any mere mortal to ever grasp, let alone explain. He is beyond the scope and capacity of any human's understanding. So it is with biblical stewardship. You always reap what you sow. You always reap more than you sow. But you will never reap a thing until you sow.

CHAPTER 11

THE LAW OF
PARTICIPATION

L ET'S NOW LOOK at the third and final principle of biblical generosity: the law of participation. I want you to read our key verse in Luke 6 again, because all three of the giving principles come out of this one verse.

> Give, and it shall be given unto you; good measure, pressed down, and shaken together, and running over, shall men give into your bosom. For with the same measure that ye mete withal it shall be measured to you again.
>
> —JESUS (LUKE 6:38)

So here are the fundamental facts of the three principles (laws). God owns everything, and I oversee what He gives me. That's the law of possession. If I do what He says with His resources, He will give it back. That's the law of promise. And if I fully participate in God's kingdom economics program, in the spirit (the "measure" in this context), I will enjoy the full blessing of the "running over," as people line up to "give into [my] bosom." You won't just get it back with interest; you'll receive the multiplied blessings of the kingdom life, as the same measure (in the spirit) that you give shall be measured (in the spirit) back to you again.

And if you don't participate in these kingdom economics, guess what? You do not get to be part of the kingdom blessing. You just don't. You're still under the law that God owns everything, and you're still under the law that God will bless you if you obey, but—as we learned in Malachi 3—if you rob God in this manner, you are cursed by a curse. God is basically saying, "If you just swallow your pride and your greed and start participating, I will move heaven and earth for you, in due season."

Through the law of participation, God is saying He will open up the windows of heaven and pack your sack to such a degree that you will not be able to contain the blessings He places upon your business, your church, your life, your ministry, your family, and your marriage. It may take a little while for it to unfold according to His plans, so just remember that you didn't get born again overnight. It's a journey. It's a refining fire. There's still some work to be done. There's still some faith to be built. You still have to right the ship in some areas, but as you are doing that, God will give you grace, and He will bless you.

GOD WANTS TO BLESS HIS CHILDREN

God wants to bless you more than you want Him to bless you. I wish the church in America understood that. God wants to bless your church more than you want Him to. He wants to grow your ministry more than you want Him to. He wants to bless your family, and He wants to bless your resources more than you want Him to. He wants to send us revival more than we are praying for it. He simply wants to bless His kids. He wants to do exceeding abundantly above all we could ever ask or think or pray or imagine (Eph. 3:20).

Stop thinking He is this mean stepdaddy up in heaven that's just waiting for you to do bad so He can hit you with a stick. He is not the punisher. No, God wants to bless His children. I'll prove that to you with the words of Jesus:

> Or what man is there of you, whom if his son ask bread, will he give him a stone? Or if he ask a fish, will he give him a serpent? If ye then, being evil, know how to give good gifts unto your children, how much more shall your Father which is in heaven give good things to them that ask him?
>
> —JESUS (MATTHEW 7:9–11)

If a father's son asked for a piece of bread, do you think that father is going to give his son a rock? Not if he is a good father. Or instead of a fish, would that daddy give his boy a snake? Not if he is a good daddy. Jesus asked in red letters— not Greg letters, but red letters—how much more shall your heavenly Father give good things to them that ask Him? If to that you say, "Well, I just don't see a lot of good things," let me tell you why. You have not because you ask not (Jas. 4:2).

When you get into the proper position of *asking*, you will get into the proper position of *receiving*. You know why God doesn't bless some people? Because the blessing would break them. Some people have not yet been stretched enough to a faith-filled capacity to handle what God wants to give them. If you are walking around with a Ziploc sandwich bag and God has wheelbarrow blessings for you, you need to be stretched before He'll pour it out. Some of you are running around with a wheelbarrow, and God's got a "beep, beep, beep" dump truck backing up in your driveway, but He's not going to spill it until you're ready for it. So don't pray for something you're not stretched and ready to receive.

LIVING OPENHANDED

If you're tithing but still clenching your fists around your resources in fear, you still need some stretching. Living open-handed does two things. First, it allows you to give out easily and freely from the resources you have, free of fear. Second, it gives God the ability to keep refilling them. Though I'm still on my journey, this is something I had to come to grips with a long time ago, especially in regard to receiving.

As noted earlier, if you're going to become a generous giver, you have to learn to be a good receiver. I'll be honest with you. I haven't done so well at receiving through the years. There was a time not too long ago when someone would try to bless me, and my first impulse was to think, "Ah, I don't want that." But God convicted me. That's why givers will say, "Don't rob me of a blessing."

If you consider yourself to be a big giver, you've got to be a big receiver as well. You have to participate at both ends of the process or you'll be blocking God's work in your life, and in others. If you struggle with receiving, you're going to have to swallow your pride, because it's not about you. If you're participating in kingdom economics, you have to obey the full program as commanded by God, because He's going to give big to you, and you cannot refuse it without refusing

God. You'd better get over yourself and learn to receive it so more can flow through you.

God wants us to keep our hands open so we can give and receive more than we can measure, so we'd better grow some bigger hands, because God wants to pack our sacks. If you're going to be an extravagant giver, you'll occasionally have to be an extravagant receiver as well. The reception of a gift can be just as important as the giving because the Bible plainly says He's going to pack our barns and burst our winepresses with blessings (Prov. 3:10).

If we don't readily receive it, we won't be able to readily give it. There's nothing spiritual about refusing to receive, and there's nothing unspiritual about learning to receive. It can be difficult and uncomfortable, no doubt, but it must be learned to fully participate in the kingdom while here on earth.

Giving is like the sponge analogy. You can fill a sponge with water, but it's not the sponge's responsibility to hold on to the water it absorbs. Its job is to use the water for a purpose other than holding on to it. But no matter how much you wring the sponge, you will never get all the water out of it. As givers, here's what God could say through this analogy: "I want to wring you out into other people, but I'm going to let you keep enough water to sustain you and your family. I'm going to ensure you keep what's needed to stay filled and blessed—moistened as it were—but I'm going to use your life to bless and spill out upon others." It's like what the old-timers say: "I'm drinking from my saucer because my cup has overflowed."

PURPOSED IN THE HEART

I want to show you the law of participation as it appears in 2 Corinthians 9. We could literally use the entirety of 2 Corinthians 8–9 in our discussion of biblical generosity as it's the longest single discourse on this subject in the New Testament. I strongly encourage you to digest those chapters in full before completing this book.

In 2 Corinthians 9, Paul writes about what we call grace giving, meaning we should be willing to give at a higher percentage under the *grace* of the gospel than anybody ever did under the Levitical law. No one under grace should ever find themselves arguing against the 10 percent tithe being the absolute minimum starting point. Let's look at a key passage in these beautiful chapters:

> But this I say, He which soweth sparingly shall reap also sparingly; and he which soweth bountifully shall reap also bountifully. Every man according as he purposeth in his heart, so let him give; not grudgingly, or of necessity: for God loveth a cheerful giver. And God is able to make all grace abound toward you; that ye, always having all sufficiency in all things, may abound to every good work.
>
> —2 CORINTHIANS 9:6–8

So here's what God is saying through Paul's pen: what you give out will determine the magnitude of the return. It's the kingdom's ROI, the biblical return on investment. You sow sparingly, you'll still get more than you had. But if you sow bountifully, you'll get gobs more—way more than what you gave.

When we read, "Every man according as he purposeth in

his heart," Paul is saying that giving is a heart issue. Earlier in this discourse, Paul said that generosity is the proof of your love—that stewardship is proof of your love for God and others (2 Cor. 8:8).

The founder of the children's home I grew up in, who died three months before I got there, said something truly profound. I never met him, but I always heard the folks there attribute this saying to him: "You can give without loving, but you can never love without giving."

Did you get that? You can give stuff away just because you have it and not love the person you're giving it to. But you can never truly love something or someone without giving to them. Do you see how that works? "Every man (gives) as he purposes in his heart." As we return to our key passage in 2 Corinthians, we see "so let him give; not grudgingly." He's definitely talking about money—where else would we see the word *grudgingly*? But let's make sure we understand that he's writing in the context of the local church.

NOT GRUDGINGLY

Folks often "grudgingly" say, "Oh great, they're taking up another offering." Why is it that everybody thinks the church should be absolutely free of any cost? Do you know what sort of people think that? The ones that don't give. Because, again, the people who complain about money are the ones who don't give at all.

The people who are generous stewards are grateful for a generous church that blesses everybody. They're also grateful that their neighbor has a bigger house than they do. If you cannot learn to rejoice in the blessings of others, don't ever ask God to bless you, because He never will. If you can't be happy that somebody has a nicer car than you, don't ever pray for a nicer car. God will never give it to you.

You'll never have the capacity to handle more until you stop wanting more for the wrong reasons. You've got to stop trying to keep up with the Joneses. God will never grow what you have if you can't rejoice in how He's growing somebody else.

Long before our current tent went up, we were a storefront church. I've been asking our church this for years and have probably asked this question five hundred times without exaggeration. What if we pray for revival, and God sends it to the church down the road? Would we be OK with that? Now I can say: I think I know why God has sent revival to Global Vision Bible Church—because we were always OK with it. All we wanted was revival in the church, no matter where it started.

If you cannot rejoice in what God is doing somewhere else, don't expect Him to do it in your vineyard. Just don't. In the same way, don't give grudgingly. Stop thinking, "Oh my goodness, I've got to give," when in fact you are so blessed that you *get to* give. That's a huge difference. But don't miss what Paul said next in 2 Corinthians 9:7: "so let him give; not grudgingly, *or of necessity*" (emphasis added). In the ESV translation it reads "or under compulsion." A lot of people give out of necessity, not from their hearts but under compulsion. They're thinking, "Well, the preacher's going to see whether I walk up or not. So I'm just going to have to give because I'll be embarrassed if I don't." If you think like that, you'd be better off not giving. If you don't mean it, don't do it.

GOD LOVES A CHEERFUL GIVER

Moving on to the next verse, as you might imagine, this is one of my favorite phrases in the whole Bible. "For God loveth a cheerful giver" (2 Cor. 9:7). Now, He'll take it from a grouchy person too, as your cash will spend like everybody else's. While God isn't at all pleased with that sort of transaction, He loves a cheerful giver. The Greek word for the phrase "cheerful giver" has lived on into the English language, and for good reason. It's *hilarium*. Does that sound familiar? God loves hilariously reckless, cheerful givers.

Pray tell me, if God loves hilarious givers, why are we so disgruntled about it? Why is the American church so happy when they're living stingy and so mad when they're being generous, when the opposite is true for God? He is not pleased with our greedy nature, but He loves and is overjoyed with a cheerful giver. When God says He *loves* something, that's huge. Don't miss that. We say, "Well, I love my dog. I love my bike. I love this speaker. I love this over here, and that over there. I love this person and even that person." We say, "I love, I love, I love." We just love to use the word *love*, and we throw it out there like it's no big deal.

But God doesn't throw words around, and He doesn't slip them into the Bible as if He has nothing better to say or is just trying to fill a gap. God says, "Let me tell you what I love: cheerful, hilarious, laughing givers." Have you ever heard somebody say, "I bet that guy's going to laugh all the way to the bank"? How about we steal that phrase and start saying, "Let's laugh all the way to the front and give!"

GOD IS ABLE

Then in verse 8 we see "and God is able to make all grace abound toward you"—watch this—"that ye, always having all sufficiency in all things, may abound to every good work." What is the abounding good work? The generosity, the things we give out. Here's what God is basically saying. "If you will be a hilarious giver, I will make sure your sack is packed so well that you will have all the resources you need for righteousness' sake. You won't do without because I can trust you, and I will make all grace abound to you in the good work that's on your heart."

Let's be honest: How many of us would like to have everything right now that we need to do what's on our heart to help other people? All of us. Right? We can all say, "There's so much I want to do for others," and mean it. God is saying, in effect, "If you'll have that mindset, here's what I will do. I will fill you up beyond your needs so that through you others can have more. I will allow you to be a PVC pipe for the kingdom. I will allow you to be a gospel-sized Jesus conduit of grace, and I will give to you to overflowing, because I know I can trust you with it. I know you will ensure it flows through you. So I will bless you so sufficiently that you can abound to every good work and make sure people around you are blessed." That's a powerful promise in the context of His love.

THE BOOMERANG PRINCIPLE

The first time I went to Australia, I had an interesting encounter with a boomerang. I'm not talking about the ones you see at Outback Steakhouse. I'm talking about a real

Outback boomerang, and the guy that showed it to me knew what he was doing with it.

I was standing in the parking lot of a church where I was preaching at a conference when this guy came outside with a boomerang in his hand. He was the real deal from head to toe and looked just like Crocodile Dundee. He was even wearing the Outback hat with the crocodile teeth on it. As he approached me, he said, "Hello, Mate. You know how to throw a boomerang?" I told him that I knew what a boomerang was but didn't know how to throw one. He said, "Let me show you, Mate." He positioned himself, and with a simple flip of his wrist he threw that boomerang all the way across the parking lot right over the cars, and before I knew it—*shwoop!*—it was back in his hand.

I said, "Give me that big boomerang, Mate." So I gripped it real good and got myself positioned, thinking, "Bring it," as if it was going to fly for me the same way. But no matter how I tried to throw it, and no matter how I positioned my hands, leaned, or prayed, I couldn't get that boomerang to fly and come back. Now, I'm the relentless type, so I did get better at it as the week progressed, and across three visits to Australia I did a little better each time, but I never got it to fly like this guy did. With virtually no effort at all, he could make that boomerang fly like a dream with just a flip of his wrist, and it always—*shwoop!*—came right back into his hand.

All that to say, I don't throw boomerangs like a pro, but I've definitely unlocked the secret to the boomerang *principle*. Here's how you unlock the boomerang principle: You pull it out. You throw it. You stand there. And it comes back to you—bigger than it was when you threw it out. With the boomerang principle, when you give, you don't know how far that thing's going to fly or how long it will be in flight, as some throws take longer than others, but there will come a moment when that boomerang will come right back into your bosom and—*shwoop!*—you'll catch it.

When you give, it shall be given. It's a fixed law that cannot be changed. That's why we should be hilarious about it. We can absolutely know it will come back to us even bigger, so the joke is on the devil. He thinks we're going to go broke. Isn't that what he keeps telling you? Rebuke that liar. The joke is on him, and he knows it. When we give our money out, God will always faithfully send it back to us so we can continue defeating the devil with even greater giving. And don't miss what this war is all about. Through our continued giving we keep emptying out his dark kingdom and sacking his evil castle so we can fill up God's kingdom and God's castle.

> Then you shall see and be radiant; your heart shall thrill and exult, because the abundance of the sea shall be turned to you, the wealth of the nations shall come to you.
>
> —ISAIAH 60:5, ESV

In the next chapter I want to switch gears and fix an old-fashioned Sunday school misnomer that has led some folks astray over the years. Are you intrigued yet? Let's dive in!

CHAPTER 12

A PLEASING AROMA: THE OFFERING BEFORE THE BLESSING

PHILIPPIANS IS ONE of those books in which Paul speaks a lot about his time in prison. When Paul came rolling into town, he didn't look for the Hilton high-rise. He looked for the local jail because he knew that in about three days he was going to be staying there. He spoke out boldly no matter what they threatened, and he paid heavily every time. It happened over and over, and eventually the Roman government cut off his head because of it. Let's take an expository look at an amazing passage in Philippians to clear up all that Sunday school confusion.

> I can do all things through Christ which strengtheneth me.
> —PHILIPPIANS 4:13

We are all familiar with this powerful verse that Paul first wrote to the church at Philippi, and through them, to all of us across history. In the context, Paul was talking about being abased—having more, having less, having a lot, having nothing—and through it all, being able to do all things through Christ, who strengthened him (and us). This is a great application to what we are talking about in this book.

Then Paul writes: "Notwithstanding ye have well done, that ye did communicate with my affliction" (v. 14). As we discussed earlier, the King James word *communicate* means *share* or *give* in this context. So Paul was essentially saying, "Notwithstanding you have done well, that you *gave* with my affliction." Then he started rolling out as an apostolic voice:

> Now ye Philippians know also, that in the beginning of the gospel, when I departed from Macedonia, no church communicated with me as concerning giving and receiving, but ye only.
> —PHILIPPIANS 4:15

Paul was saying in effect, "Nobody believed in what I was doing. Nobody helped me, even as I suffered. Nobody supported me as a church planter, a young pastor, an evangelist, a missionary, an apostle, nothing." Then look closely at the end of the verse: "*...but ye only.*"

He was saying, "When I started this journey, I made note of who paid the bills to put up the first tent. No church gave at all, no church took up an offering for me, *but you only*. You, church at Philippi, you were the first to give."

Then Paul wrote, "For even in Thessalonica ye sent once

and again unto my necessity" (v. 16). In saying "once and again," he's making note that they actually gave twice before anyone else did. He was saying, "You found out I was suffering through some problems. You found out I'd been in prison. You found out I had some needs and some bills that were going unpaid, and you gave not once but twice to meet my needs, while no other church did." Now watch in verse 17 where he hits on the promise:

> Not because I desire a gift: but I desire fruit that may
> abound to your account.
>
> —PHILIPPIANS 4:17

Paul was saying, "Do you know why it was needful for you to send me money? It wasn't just because I needed the money, but because *you needed* to send it. Because when you sent it, God recorded in heaven to your account that you gave to my needs when nobody else would." Paul didn't just desire their help, he wanted to ensure they realized that this giving would store up for them treasure in heaven, just as Jesus commanded—and promised. Then he wrote:

> But I have all, and abound: I am full, having received
> of Epaphroditus the things which were sent from you,
> an odour of a sweet smell, a sacrifice acceptable, well-
> pleasing to God.
>
> —PHILIPPIANS 4:18

Epaphroditus was the man who brought him the offering, so Paul was saying, "I received the offerings. I received the money. I received what I needed. Epaphroditus brought it to me." Now, here's where we need to correct some confusion.

He called it "an odor of a sweet smell, a sacrifice acceptable, wellpleasing to God."

I'm not going to start a whole theological debate on this, but here's how Christians normally read that phrase. In fact, when I was in seminary, here's how the teachers would say this passage actually reads: Paul's in jail. The church takes up money. Then they send it to Epaphroditus, and somehow Epaphroditus uses the money to buy some perfume. And Paul says, "I want to thank you for this sweet-smelling gift you gave me."

Maybe they got that impression from Mary's extravagant act of pouring out her expensive ointment onto Jesus, as we studied earlier, but that would be a very poor interpretation of Paul's letter to the Philippians. In the Book of Exodus, God said the offerings that were pleasing to Him were "a pleasing aroma" (Exod. 29:18, ESV). When He said this, He was directly referencing a violent blood sacrifice, an offering at the altar that was a sweet-smelling odor in His nostrils, as He required a sacrificial *offering before the blessing*.

So Paul said, "When you sent me what you did, it was a sweet-smelling odor, a sacrifice." To whom was he saying it was pleasing? To Paul himself? No, but to God. Paul is sitting in jail, and Epaphroditus brings him a love offering from the church at Philippi. So Paul is thinking, "Hallelujah...I have some needs that can be met now. Thank You, Lord." And the Lord says, "That's a pleasant aroma to me." In all our giving, it is always primarily unto the Lord and never just to meet the needs of the people. When giving sacrificially, we must never forget to whom we offer *all* our worship and praise.

THE OFFERING BEFORE THE BLESSING

I was in Colombia for a conference a few months before writing this book. While there, my dear friend Prophet Gustavo and I visited a museum together, and I quickly recognized there's more gold in Colombia than I had ever seen in my life—and I've traveled the entire world. This museum was literally packed with gold stuff, so much so that the vault doors were as thick as an upright piano, and the security technology was very impressive.

On our tour through the museum, we went into a massive room that was a reconstruction of an Aztec chamber of sacrifice. They even had mannequins set up that depicted a sacrificial ceremony, as conducted by the Aztecs and Mayans. Every symbol and artifact on the walls of this chamber was all about the devil—it was some very weird and very dark stuff.

Even so, in the context of a museum, I found it all to be quite interesting. At one point, with Prophet Gustavo talking through an interpreter, he said, "Isn't it interesting, Pastor Locke, that even the devil understands the principle of the offering before the blessing." And there it is.

That's why the devil wants to steal your seed and your offering. Even the kingdom of darkness understands the power of the offering system. Even satanists know how to get the blessing of power and influence. They know they have to make an offering to their god. Yet somehow the church doesn't understand this, as most are too busy offering to their own flesh and other demonized idols. If that's you, please realize that the devil—the devourer—has hijacked your offering.

Returning to our key passage in Philippians, we see that the people gave their offering to Paul while he was sitting in a jail cell, and God basically said, "I am pleased with the smell of the offering you have given to the man of God." It's important to note that other passages of Scripture reveal that these churches were not rich megachurches. They may have been relatively large, but they were broke because they were under the tyranny and persecution of the Roman government and had been driven underground. They typically met secretly from house to house, and in some instances they were even meeting out in the woods.

There's no doubt that what they gave was, as the Bible says, "a sacrifice." These people gave, and it was a legitimate *love* offering. In modern Christianity we also call them "love offerings," but most offerings that come from the American church are just offerings, as there's no real *love* behind the giving. Most of the people doing the giving today don't even like the people receiving. In contrast, these people gave sacrificially because they *loved*. And because they did, Paul knew something that, in context, God is trying to explain to us. He knew the people at Philippi would be thinking, "Wow! We gave to the man of God. We hope it was a blessing to him. But what are we going to do now? We don't have much to go around. Nonetheless, we gave our hard-earned resources, not grudgingly or out of necessity, because we know God loves a cheerful giver, so we'll just have to figure it out."

When Paul wrote back to them after receiving their gift, as we see in this letter that we now call the Book of Philippians, he challenged this way of thinking. When you pastor people long enough, you know how they're thinking sometimes even before they're thinking it. I often know how people will respond before they give the response. People often say I preach based on the people's response, when in fact I preach based on how I hope you'll respond—and there's a big difference. So Paul knew when and where he was going to land this beautiful message to the church as he did with what he wrote next:

> But my God shall supply all your need according to his
> riches in glory by Christ Jesus.
> —PHILIPPIANS 4:19

I'll never have an unpaid bill that has God's name on it, because "my God shall supply all my needs according to His riches in glory by Christ Jesus." Make sure when you quote that verse, you're living it, because the only reason Paul gave *them* the assurance of verse 19 was because of what they did in verses 14–18. Don't miss this.

You do not get to claim Philippians 4:19 in your life if you are not living Philippians 4:14–18. If you're not a sacrificial giver living in obedience to the kingdom of God, do not expect this blessing. Philippians 4:19 is written only for those walking in the *gift of giving*, and it is truly a *gift* from God (Rom. 12:8).

Many people want to quote Philippians 4:19 and then say, "Well, I've been speaking Philippians 4:19 over my life, and it just ain't working." Remember this: you can only claim what you live. The promise is there forever, but you must first appropriate it through your giving to make it true in your life.

Everybody wants to quote the Bible when it's convenient for them, but virtually nobody wants to live it when it's talking about sacrificial living. Everybody wants to talk about a book they believe in, but for the vast majority it's not a book they *behave*. If we are not biblically generous, how dare we quote the Scriptures or sing the songs that say, "I'm living my life in the image of Christ." Are you?

Jesus Takes Care of Our Needs

Jesus wasn't stingy, and He could have been. Jesus wasn't miserly or materialistic or selfish. He gave of Himself all the way to the cross. Jesus said in effect, "If somebody asks you for something, and you have it beside you, don't say, 'Come back tomorrow, and I'll give it to you.' Give it to them right then and there" (Prov. 3:28). He also told us that if a brother or sister needs money, to give it to them expecting nothing in return (Luke 6:34–35).

We obviously know Jesus could have done a lot of things with money, but He didn't. Instead, He taught us how to give it away. He taught us how to bless others with it, because that's what He did. He taught us that the only remedy to materialism and greed is biblical generosity. You simply can't serve God and mammon. In this context, let's take another look at Jesus' fundamental message on money from the Sermon on the Mount in Matthew 6. He said not to lay up for yourselves treasures on earth but to lay up for yourselves treasures in heaven, for where your treasure is, there will your heart be also. Jesus was saying in effect, "You simply can't truly love or serve Me if you love your stuff and are always worried about money" (Matt. 6:19–24). From there, He promises to take care of our *every* need here on earth.

> Therefore I tell you, do not be anxious about your life, what you will eat or what you will drink, nor about your body, what you will put on. Is not life more than food, and the body more than clothing?
>
> —Matthew 6:25, esv

Could there be a clearer command not to worry about your resources? Remember, that's in the red letters of the Bible, straight out of the mouth of God.

Then Jesus says, "Just in case you're worried about *how* I'm going to take care of you, look at the birds of the air. I take care of every single bird. Are you not much better than a bird? Are you not better than flowers? Are you not better than grass? Are you not better than the bugs? Are you not better than the things of nature? I take care of all of it, so you can know that I'm going to take care of you too. And here's all you have to do: seek first the kingdom of God and His righteousness. Do that, and I'll take care of tomorrow. Do what's right today, and I'll take care of your every need" (Matt. 6:24–34).

In the context of this incredibly beautiful message, do you know what Jesus is talking about? Your mammon. Your stuff. Your resources. He's telling you that if you will be generous with what God has given you, you'll never have to worry about these three things: food, clothes, and a roof over your head. You may not have the extravagance the enemy baits you to want, but if you will seek first the kingdom of God and His righteousness, He will make sure you have all the *things* (food, clothes, and shelter) you actually need.

We often think the things we want *are* the things we need. But God knows better. Some of us act like God is an Amazon wish list. We've got to stop that foolishness. He said, "If you will be faithful with putting Me first, I'll make sure you have the basic necessities of life." Now, just as we discussed earlier, God will undoubtedly bless you *over and abundantly* at times to give you way more than you feel you deserve. Praise God for that.

Here's the problem that will usually arise. If we *want* for the extra so much, it will start to feel like a need, and then we will start seeking the extra and literally miss God. We will eventually lose the very thing we're supposed to be seeking. Don't risk that. The Bible is teaching us that if you will simply get in line with God's program of giving generously to others, He will bless you unbelievably, and you will never lack in times of need.

CHAPTER 13

THE PARADOX
OF RICHES

N OW LET'S FURTHER discuss one of the greatest principles in the Bible. In delivering it, God enters through the back door to describe this principle in a beautifully poetic way. Proverbs is the book of wisdom, and oh, how we need more of that. Proverbs 1:5 says, "A wise man will hear, and will increase learning," which parallels well with James 1:5, "If any of you lacks wisdom, let him ask God, who gives generously to all without reproach, and it will be given him" (ESV).

As we discussed earlier, Solomon penned all the proverbs for God, and as one might expect from the wisest man who ever lived, he had more money and more street smarts than any person who will ever live. God said there will never be another man like him (1 Kings 3:12). You take Bill Gates, Warren Buffett, Jeff Bezos, Mark Zuckerberg, and Elon

Musk and roll all their money into one bank account, and it wouldn't even touch the wealth that Solomon had at his fingertips. Let that sink in.

How do we know this? Because God said so. God said he's the richest man to ever walk the earth or ever will walk the earth (2 Chron. 1:12). That's rich beyond any golden imagination. Keep that firmly in mind as we study one of the most powerful Bible paradoxes he penned.

> There is that maketh himself rich, yet hath nothing: there
> is that maketh himself poor, yet hath great riches.
>   —PROVERBS 13:7

Talk about opposites attracting. At first blush, this proverb seems very odd, especially coming from the guy who had more money than any of us could even imagine or pray for. Solomon is saying there are people who take their money and store it up to make themselves feel rich. And do you know what they have? Nothing but problems and nothing to show for it except a pretty bank account. They make themselves feel and even appear rich in superficial ways, but they really have nothing.

Then there are those who intentionally make themselves poor because rather than storing up for the purpose of storing up, they stay busy giving out. They give out so much it seems like they're going to be put in the poorhouse, so to speak, but that will never happen. Not a chance. You see, if you hoard it, you end up having a lot of pretty numbers in your bank account but nothing in life that matters.

Let's prove that. You can go to any bank in America right now and run into this telling reality. Say you had millions of dollars in your account and went up to the teller to take out a large chunk of cash. Do you know what the bank would say? "Oh, we don't keep money like that on hand."

Recently we gave a Mother's Day blessing to all the single moms in our community, and we wanted to give them all a large sum of cash in an envelope rather than a check. You wouldn't believe how difficult it was for me to get the actual cash money out of our bank. When I started hitting walls, I said, "Excuse me, you have a vault right over there as big as my bedroom. Can't you just bring out some cash?" And the teller answered, "No, we have to order large amounts of cash like that." Then I asked, "So you're telling me that everything that's in everybody's account is really just a number?" And, of course, the answer was, "Yes."

Your bank is in the business of loaning out the money you have stored up in your bank account, and it's not actually keeping it in a safe for you. It's all just a bunch of digits in the digital domain.

FIFTEEN MORE YEARS

A friend of mine is so rich he doesn't even know what to do with all his money. This man is worth $50 million on a bad day, and he's a good case study for this book for one reason. Knowing that he's my friend and someone who has enjoyed my preaching over the years, it may surprise you to learn that he struggles to give any of it away. He's just letting those numbers grow and grow and grow. And when he does spend it, there always has to be real value attached, so even his stuff can grow and grow and grow those numbers.

I baptized him, he made his public profession of faith in my office, and we've also discussed the aforementioned lawsuits against us. As for the big question you're surely asking by now, the answer is yes. I've been bold with him about sowing into the kingdom, and he always says, "Not right now." But on one occasion he did approach me and say, "Here's $500 for the church, Son."

What got him coming to Global Vision in the first place was a big spot of cancer that broke out on his forehead, and someone told him, "Go to Greg Locke's church. They'll pray over you."

After a couple of weeks of attending our services, he approached me in the tent and told me about his condition. He said, "I want you to pray over me, that God would heal me. You remember that guy in the Bible named Hezekiah?" I said, "Yeah, I know who Hezekiah is." Then he said, "That prophet Isaiah prayed over him, and God gave him fifteen more years. Do you think you can pray that God gives me fifteen more years?"

"Well, I'm no prophet Isaiah," I said, "but I'll try." To my surprise, he knelt down in the wood shavings we had as our floor back then. I laid my hand on his forehead, the richest man I knew. Silver and gold, I had none. But what I did have, I gave freely. I just laid my hand on his head and prayed in the name of Jesus.

He came back the next week and had some stitches on his head. So I called out to him and asked, "You alright?" He said, "Alright. I went back to the doctor, and they stitched up that hole. Then they started doing scans on my head and all that stuff, Preacher. I'll be if you ain't like Isaiah. I ain't got a lick of cancer in that spot on my forehead anymore. I believe God's going to give me fifteen more years, Son." To which I said, "I pray God will give you forty."

This man had more numbers in the bank than most would

ever dream of, but he didn't have more years. Notice that he didn't ask me to pray for more money. He asked me to pray for more time. You can find yourself with all the money you could ever want and have no time left to spend it on others. Let me put a twist on a well-known (though incorrect) cliché. He that dies with the most toys still dies. There are people who make themselves rich, but they have nothing. Then there are those who live their lives in a way that can make them seem poor, just so they can freely give to others.

You always reap what you sow.

You always reap more than you sow.

You never reap a thing until you sow.

It's the principle of sowing and reaping, and it's a law that will never change. The people who live their lives to hoard up wealth will have nothing to show for it in the end. But the people who live their lives freely, openhanded, openhearted, giving it all away, are the most blessed people on the planet—in this life and far more in the next.

I will never give up hope that this man will see the light concerning his giving, so I will pray for him always, counsel him when he asks, and boldly encourage him at every opportunity. While I choose to believe he will eventually turn around, even if it takes fifteen years, I'll let Jesus close this story in the most pressing way possible. It's a story about a man who had it all but never learned to give.

> And he told them a parable, saying, "The land of a rich man produced plentifully, and he thought to himself, 'What shall I do, for I have nowhere to store my crops?' And he said, 'I will do this: I will tear down my barns and build larger ones, and there I will store all my grain and my goods. And I will say to my soul, "Soul, you have

ample goods laid up for many years; relax, eat, drink, be merry.'" But God said to him, 'Fool! This night your soul is required of you, and the things you have prepared, whose will they be?' So is the one who lays up treasure for himself and is not rich toward God."

—LUKE 12:16–21, ESV

MOTIVATIONAL GIFTS

As I mentioned earlier, giving is a gift of the Spirit, as we learn in Romans 12, which is all about surrender. Three times in the Bible spiritual gifts are discussed explicitly, and the group in Romans 12 are called the motivation gifts, as these seven gifts serve to motivate the body of Christ. Next we find the nine manifestation gifts in 1 Corinthians 12. And finally we have the fivefold gifts to the church in Ephesians 4. I wrote extensively on the gifts of the Spirit in my book *Accessing Your Anointing*, so I strongly encourage you to read it if you haven't already.

All gifts have a single purpose: "For the perfecting of the saints, for the work of the ministry, for the edifying of the body of Christ" (Eph. 4:12). Your gifts are not for you. Your gifts are meant to glorify God and bless and benefit those around you. If you use your gifts wisely, you'll probably make your boss a lot of money, but you weren't given a gift for that purpose. You were given gifts so that you could empty out hell and fill up heaven. That's why you were given your gifts. Let's dig in to see where the gift of giving is identified:

> Having then gifts differing according to the grace that is given to us, whether prophecy, let us prophesy according to the proportion of faith; or ministry, let us wait on our ministering: or he that teacheth, on teaching; or he that

exhorteth, on exhortation: he that giveth, let him do it
with simplicity.

—ROMANS 12:6–8

When Paul said we are to give "with simplicity," here's what
he meant. We can try to spiritualize it or even dumb it down,
but it's as simple as the Word says it is. If I really have the
gift of giving, it will be as simple as it is for me to walk up
on this platform, grab a microphone, and talk. That's not at
all difficult for me. It comes naturally, so I can do it without
much thought. That's how simple it should be for me to write
checks and give money away.

Folks who have the gift of generosity do it simplistically.
In my own life, I don't lose sleep over giving. I never second-
guess myself. My wife never argues or tries to talk me out of
it. At most she'll say, "If that's what the Holy Ghost told you
to give, give it. Give it all. Put another zero. Who cares? Burn
the barn down. God will build a bigger one." If you have this
gift, it's easy for you to be a hilarious, laughing giver, and
you will never sweat over it. You will live your life looking for
opportunities to bless people. That's what it means to give
with simplicity. It's just what you want to do.

GIVING IS THE KEY

I find it fascinating that among the supernatural gifts of God,
He includes giving. Do you know what giving will do for
you, even beyond God's refilling? It will unlock supernatural
doors in your life. Remember the act that sent us into revival
at Global Vision—our act of sacrificial, extravagant generosity to the Wonser family when we were at our lowest point
financially? That turnaround was supernatural, and it happened with simplicity.

I'm not going to tell you God is going to make you a millionaire, no matter how much you give. He might, but that shouldn't be your goal anyway. What I am saying is that if you give out of a heart of earnest love for God and others in the natural realm, God will open up the atmosphere of the supernatural and pour down kingdom blessings upon you— blessings you could never imagine are possible. Giving will unlock the supernatural in your life like nothing else can. It's a simple fact. Giving is the key to God's blessings in your life, and nothing will change your life more than biblical generosity. Likewise, when God can trust you to give of your gifts, He will bless you with more than you can imagine.

When God sees that He can trust you with that business, He's going to bless that business beyond measure, because He knows the end result. He knows you are going to use that business for the glory of God and the furtherance of His kingdom. Likewise, when He sees that He can trust your church, He's going to bless that church beyond imagination. You see, not every church is blessed by God because not every church is trusted by God. We have to put ourselves in a position of trustworthiness in our stewardship so God can say, "Well done, good and faithful servant. You have been faithful over a little; I will set you over much" (Matt. 25:21, ESV).

There's only one context in the Bible in which God uses the phrase, "Well done, good and faithful servant." It's used a couple of times in related passages in the Gospels, but it is always in the same context. The way folks overuse that phrase would lead you to think it's found all throughout the Bible, as if Jesus was always going around saying, "Well done, well done!" No. It is only found in one context in the Bible.

We most often hear it preached like this: "When we get to

heaven—when we stand before the judgment seat of Christ—we will hear, 'Well done, thou good and faithful servant.'" But the only people who will hear "well done" are those that did well in one area: giving.

Let's see how Jesus actually used that phrase in His Olivet Discourse, the very week He went to the cross. This sermon got that name because He taught it on the Mount of Olives. As you read, please note that a talent was about seventy-five pounds of gold, as that was a common measurement which most historians believe was based on the weight an average man could carry. If you're curious, just one talent of gold is worth well over a million dollars today. This is the parable of the talents:

> For it will be like a man going on a journey, who called his servants and entrusted to them his property. To one he gave five talents, to another two, to another one, to each according to his ability. Then he went away. He who had received the five talents went at once and traded with them, and he made five talents more. So also he who had the two talents made two talents more. But he who had received the one talent went and dug in the ground and hid his master's money. Now after a long time the master of those servants came and settled accounts with them. And he who had received the five talents came forward, bringing five talents more, saying, "Master, you delivered to me five talents; here, I have made five talents more." His master said to him, "Well done, good and faithful servant. You have been faithful over a little; I will set you over much. Enter into the joy of your master." And he also who had the two talents came forward, saying, "Master, you delivered to me two talents; here, I have made two talents more." His master said to him, "Well done, good

and faithful servant. You have been faithful over a little; I
will set you over much. Enter into the joy of your master."
—JESUS (MATTHEW 25:14–23, ESV)

As we pause the parable midstream, please recognize that
this is a passage about stewardship. Remember, every verse
in the Bible can have multiple applications but just one
interpretation in the context, and this one is about money.
So take a big gulp and take this to heart, as here is what
Jesus is saying: if you are a kingdom-minded, born-again
believer—a righteously resourced steward—one day you
will be in His presence, and you will hear the phrase, "Well
done, thou good and faithful servant," because you used His
money as a tool to build the kingdom, and you were not the
servant of money. Now, do you know what He says to those
who do not do well in their stewardship? Let's continue in
the parable to see.

> He also who had received the one talent came forward,
> saying, "Master, I knew you to be a hard man, reaping
> where you did not sow, and gathering where you scat-
> tered no seed, so I was afraid, and I went and hid your
> talent in the ground. Here, you have what is yours." But
> his master answered him, "You wicked and slothful ser-
> vant! You knew that I reap where I have not sown and
> gather where I scattered no seed? Then you ought to have
> invested my money with the bankers, and at my coming I
> should have received what was my own with interest. So
> take the talent from him and give it to him who has the
> ten talents. For to everyone who has will more be given,
> and he will have an abundance. But from the one who
> has not, even what he has will be taken away. And cast

the worthless servant into the outer darkness. In that
place there will be weeping and gnashing of teeth."
—Jesus (Matthew 25:24–30, esv)

Jesus is saying in the context, "If you are not a good
steward—if you are not a good and faithful and obedient
servant—you will be cast into outer darkness, where there
will be weeping and gnashing of teeth." I'm pretty sure you
never heard that preached on Easter. I'm being very careful
how I phrase this next sentence, so brace yourself. In this
profound parable, Jesus is basically saying there is nothing we
can do to get saved, but there are things we will do because
we are saved. Let me explain.

Earlier in this same discourse on the Mount of Olives, Jesus
told us that those who endure to the end shall be saved (Matt.
24:13). Is He saying that we have to work and work and work
to be saved? No. Rather, He's saying you will work *because*
you are saved. You will *endure* because you are saved. You
will *give* because you are saved. Or, as Paul put it, you will
work out your own salvation with fear and trembling toward
the Lord (Phil. 2:12). You will work out what God has worked
into you—you will work with that which God has given you.

Those who are truly born again and understand what the
gospel is about, those who have received the extravagant gift
of God's forgiveness, will not live their lives in a stingy, greedy,
self-absorbed, self-advancing way—nor in sloth. Through this
parable Jesus is telling us a simple, piercing truth. The condition of your heart will be revealed through your stewardship.
If your heart is selfish and greedy—in love with money and
the servant of it—it is an indication that it has never truly
been saved by God's grace.

You will never meet a Holy Spirit–filled believer that is mad

about obedience to the principles of God, least of all generosity. You just won't. And when God says, "Well done, thou
good and faithful servant," as He does in this parable, it will
be because of your giving.

All this can be kind of unnerving, right? In an era of sloppy
salvation, the red letter words of Jesus can do that to us. We
can write songs about it, and we can write books about it,
but no matter what you've heard—according to God—the
only people who will hear the phrase "Well done, thou good
and faithful servant" are the ones who are faithful with the
resources He puts in their hands.

SPIRITUAL ROI

Notice in the parable that the good and faithful servants were
able to take the resources and invest them; thus the kingdom
expanded. When the king came back, He said in effect,
"You've done well. You're a good and faithful servant. So I'm
not just going to let you keep what you've made; I'm also going
to give you more, because I know I can trust you to reinvest
it, and you're going to make more and more and more for the
kingdom." God's big on spiritual ROI—the return on investment for His kingdom.

I don't know about you, but I want to live my life here on
earth in such an extravagantly generous way that—though it
may make everybody around me uncomfortable and cause
the entire world and even the church at large to misunder-
stand me—I'm going to give till it hurts, and I'm going to
obey what the Word of God says. I'm not living for man's
approval but only for God's, so I am going to be a biblically
generous person with every single thing God has given me.
I'm going to invest it back into the kingdom, with simplicity.

I'm going to do all I can to show He can trust me so I may know without a doubt that He will greatly bless me. Knowing all the Lord has said on this subject, what else would I do?

> Learn to do well; seek judgment, relieve the oppressed, judge the fatherless, plead for the widow. Come now, and let us reason together, saith the LORD: though your sins be as scarlet, they shall be as white as snow; though they be red like crimson, they shall be as wool. If ye be willing and obedient, ye shall eat the good of the land: But if ye refuse and rebel, ye shall be devoured with the sword: for the mouth of the LORD hath spoken it.
>
> —ISAIAH 1:17–20

A HALLELUJAH VOICEMAIL

D. R. Harrison, a dear friend and evangelist that launched his ministry out of our church, has navigated the twists and turns of his own personal journey for quite a while now, and it has been inspiring to watch. I was recently teaching at our conference on the subject of biblical generosity in preparation for this book, and D. R. was preaching at a series of Lutheran churches up in South Dakota at the same time. While I was between teaching sessions, he sent me a long voicemail to testify something I'm sure the Holy Spirit knew would charge me up before I began to teach the next session.

He said, "Pastor Locke, we are seeing things up here that we've never seen before. Last night, people started coming forward and getting saved. The spirit of religion just started coming off of these people, and they started manifesting unforgiveness all over the place. It's truly unbelievable."

Then he said, "People like elders, deacons, Sunday school teachers, people that have been in this church for years, just started getting up, impromptu, bringing tithes to the altar. I've never seen anything like it, and I wasn't even preaching on generosity or giving. God just started touching these people's hearts. They just started coming up to the altar paying years in back tithes and bringing cash up to the altar. I just want to thank you as my pastor for leading the way."

The kicker came when he said he was sitting there taking it all in when the Holy Spirit said, "See that preacher over there?" D. R. didn't know the first thing about the preacher, but it turned out he was the main pastor of one of the Lutheran churches that was part of the gathering. This man has seven kids, and D. R. discovered that he drove a station wagon with 400,000 miles on it. He sensed the Holy Spirit telling him to rebuke those people for treating their pastor that way.

So D. R. got up, grabbed the microphone, and said, "Look, I'm not trying to hurt anybody's feelings, but if I have to, I have to. Look what God is doing. Generosity is breaking out in this place." Then, looking at the pastor that God highlighted, he said, "Man of God, stand up. Some of you here are driving $80,000 SUVs, and this man has a station wagon that has 400,000 miles on it. He's also got seven kids and can barely pay his bills. Now he's having to work two jobs to make ends meet. But we're going to do something about that right now."

Then D. R. asked, "How much is the honorarium that you were going to give me?" One of the host pastors answered, "We're going to give you $2,000." To which D. R. said, "Alright, I'm going to put it in the bucket. I'm going to start an offering to get this man a car."

He continued on the voicemail, "So I'm standing there, and people are whispering amongst themselves, but it was so quiet you could've heard a gnat burp. The Holy Spirit told me, 'Tell them, if you all don't step up and help this man get a new car, my wife and I will make it happen over the course of this next month.' Something shifted when I got bold with them like that. And in less than five minutes, people laid $62,000 on the altar to buy that pastor a brand-new SUV for his family."

D. R. closed this six-and-a-half-minute voicemail saying, "Pastor, I'm telling you all this to say thank you for teaching me about extravagant generosity. I've seen what happens with my own eyes when you obey God at all costs and simply leave the consequences up to Him. It's beautiful to behold."

As I listened to that, all I could say was, "Yes, it is. Thank You, Lord." After two very long teaching sessions and another one to go, I was running on fumes—and God knew. When we operate in biblical generosity, He is always going to meet our every need, and then some. Can you imagine how that voicemail blessed that final session? It practically lifted me onto the platform. Thank You, again and again, Lord, and thank you for your obedience, D. R. Harrison. Well done.

CHAPTER 14

SPARKING REVIVAL FIRE

I BELIEVE D. R.'S STORY in the last chapter sets me up beautifully for what I now want to discuss, revival giving, and here's why: every major move of God can be marked by the generosity of God's people. If a church experiences any level of Holy Spirit awakening, you can be sure of one thing—that church (or family or community or individual) will experience uncomfortably radical levels of extravagant generosity. Imagine the discomfort that went through that room after D. R. called out the people, and imagine how that, in turn, brought him and his wife (not to mention the host pastor's team) an even higher level of discomfort.

It's unavoidable, and there is no exception to that rule. The radical giving we currently experience in our church is the result of the revival we're experiencing, and that revival—as you now know—was the result of our extravagant giving. The presence of the Holy Spirit is incredibly strong in our church, and we know firsthand why that is. If a particular church wants revival, it will first have to break out of stinginess. Otherwise it's impossible. History is filled to overflowing with examples of that.

I'm not the greatest revival historian there is, but I did write my master's thesis on revival—not just in America but around the world. I also took that thesis as the raw material to write my book on revival, simply titled *Revival*. I'm definitely drawn to all things relating to biblical revival. I've even named my kids (and my dog) after great revivalists. I know the dates, the facts, the figures. I've even got some revival memorabilia in my office right now, in my little makeshift museum that I'm putting together.

I have deeply studied the great revivals from history— the First Great Awakening, the Second Great Awakening, the Hebrides Revival, Jeremiah Calvin Lanphier's New York Revival, and the Welsh Revival of 1904–1905 where two million people were swept into the kingdom of God. From my study of these and many more, I can tell you with complete certainty that every revival in the history of the world was sparked and marked by one thing, and that's radical giving.

THREE BIBLICAL REVIVALS

If people's hearts and pocketbooks are not loosened, you can call it a cute meeting where people got emotionally supercharged, but you can never call it revival. Real awakening always stirs biblical generosity—unbelievably radical levels of biblical generosity. The Bible proves that better than I can, so let's take a look at three biblical revivals, two instances from the Old Testament and one from the New Testament.

In Exodus 25, we see that Moses is on the mountaintop with God. In that mountaintop encounter, God is telling him in effect, "This is what I want the tabernacle to look like, and these are the specific dimensions and materials I want you to use to build the ark of the covenant, which is the testimony of God" (Exod. 25:1–22, paraphrased).

God gives Moses a lot of specifics, so we know numbers, lengths, and widths are extremely important to God. These are not just insignificant details to be overlooked in the Bible. Everything God says is important. To make all His instructions come to fruition, the people were going to have to bring a freewill offering from their hands to Moses, the man of God.

The question now is, How were these people—former slaves who were wandering in the wilderness at the time—going to be able to bring these things to Moses? On a handful of occasions, the Bible says that God gave His people favor with the Egyptians, so they took great spoils from Egypt when they left (Exod. 12:36). So they basically borrowed from their neighbors with no requirement to pay them back. God gave them favor, and they rolled out of Egypt with wagons and chariots and wheelbarrows full of stuff.

Now, with all that in mind, we then see Moses calling on the leaders and the people. You always start with the leadership, because if they're not giving, the people will never become givers. Moses gets them together and basically says, "Look, we need to bring a freewill offering to God so we will have the materials needed to build everything that God just gave me the blueprints to build." Blueprints to a leader are worthless if you don't have follow-through from the people you're leading, right?

As a leader, I can have every vision in the world, but if God's people sit on His money and do nothing with it, the vision will never come to pass. It never comes to fruition. So watch what happens in Exodus 36:

> Then wrought Bezaleel and Aholihab, and every wise hearted man, in whom the LORD put wisdom and understanding to know how to work all manner of work for the service of the sanctuary, according to all that the Lord had commanded.
>
> —EXODUS 36:1–3

Here's one of my favorite people in the Bible, though he is so often overlooked—Bezaleel. In another passage of Scripture, he was the first person in the Bible to be full of the Holy Spirit as he was called to build the ark of the covenant. You'd better be filled with the Holy Spirit if you start building a structure for God to dwell in. As we continue in chapter 36, we see:

> And Moses called Bezaleel and Aholiab, and every wise hearted man, in whose heart the LORD had put wisdom, even every one whose heart stirred him up to come unto the work to do it: And they received of Moses all the offering, which the children of Israel had brought for the work of the service of the sanctuary, to make it withal. And they brought yet unto him free offerings every morning.
>
> —EXODUS 36:2–3

The people just kept bringing it, bringing it, and bringing it. Then the Bible says:

> And all the wise men, that wrought all the work of the sanctuary, came every man from his work which they made; and they spake unto Moses, saying, The people bring much more than enough for the service of the work, which the LORD commanded to make.
>
> —EXODUS 36:4–5

THE TOO MUCH REVIVAL

With that rich visual backdrop for our first example of biblical revival, which we can call the Too Much Revival, let's discuss where it gets its name: the *too much* offering of Exodus 36:6. Have you ever heard of one of those? It's when a preacher gets up and says, "Whoa, we have too much! Let's stop it right there and not take up anymore." You've never heard that, and you probably never will. But this was the historic *too much* offering, and this is the revival that took place.

> And Moses gave commandment, and they caused it to be proclaimed throughout the camp, saying, Let neither man nor woman make any more work for the offering of the sanctuary. So the people were restrained from bringing.
>
> —EXODUS 36:6

Moses said, "We've got too much surplus to build what God told us to build, so let's just cut it off right here." As a result, the people were restrained from giving. I love this next verse.

> For the stuff they had was sufficient for all the work to make it, and too much.
>
> —EXODUS 36:7

There's our namesake verse for the "too much offering" in the Bible. When your heart is stirred up for the things of God, we call that revival. And when your heart is stirred, generosity is a natural biblical outpouring.

The people brought and brought and brought, and by bringing in this way, they brought down the presence of God. Let's be reminded of what we established earlier: the offering comes before the blessing. Their hearts were stirred, they brought their radical offering, and God's glory showed up and shocked them.

And just like us today, the people were *off and on*. They were a little hot here, a little cold there, and a little lukewarm at times. Moses dealt with all that. But at the end of the day, this was a picture of what the *too much offering* looked like so we can aspire to it today.

The sacrificial obedience these people exhibited was on a level of excellence that we could never imagine in the local church in America today, but we can hope for it. Moses literally had to get up and say, under Holy Spirit inspiration, "We've got too much." Can you imagine having that sort of spiritual problem today? I can.

HEZEKIAH'S REVIVAL

Our next example is also mentioned in the Book of Kings, but we're going to deal with this particular aspect of it as we read in 2 Chronicles 31. This revival helps build the case that when real revival takes place, real generosity is always on the forefront of what is happening—every single time.

You'll notice that the words "the king did that which was evil in the sight of the Lord" is a recurring theme in the Bible. Over and over we read that about the kings of the Old

Testament, as only about six of them did that which was right in the sight of the Lord, and two of them were more righteous than any of the rest: Josiah and Hezekiah.

Hezekiah was a man that sought after God with great boldness and intensity. When he got a letter from another government saying, "We're coming to destroy you," the Bible says he took that letter up to the house of God and spread it before the Lord, where he basically cried out, "Lord, You see what they've written about us. Please do something about it." And God stepped off His throne and did something about it. God killed those people (2 Kings 19:14–37).

Even more, the Bible tells us that within the first month of his reign, Hezekiah started tearing down the high places of idolatry. He killed the prophets of Baal. He took care of the wicked priests that were offering oblations to false gods. Please make note that in the Old Testament little G "gods" are literal demons. So these priests were offering to demons. Hezekiah cleaned house.

The Bible also tells us Hezekiah went into the house of God and took out all the rubbish. Isn't that interesting? The house of God had lain in waste while the priests lived in their extravagance. The temple was so full of filth that it looked like a trash dump. So Hezekiah said, "You clean that place out now, and you'd better hope the glory of God doesn't fall and consume you for letting trash build up in His house." So the people immediately began to clear out the house of God to make room for the presence of God that was soon to come (2 Chron. 29:3–31).

From there, Hezekiah started praying, fasting, and putting on sackcloth. This man was dead earnest in his obedience to God, and he wanted to see revival in ways that we could never imagine, but we should be doing the same. If we really want to see and experience a move of God in both the church and our own personal lives, we should be equally earnest in our obedience. Then in verse 4 of this powerful chapter we see an aspect of the revival that I think is among the most important:

> Moreover he commanded the people that dwelt in Jerusalem to give the portion of the priests and the Levites, that they might be encouraged in the law of the LORD. And as soon as the commandment came abroad, the children of Israel brought in abundance the firstfruits of corn, wine, and oil, and honey, and of all the increase of the field; and the tithe of all things brought they in abundantly.
>
> —2 CHRONICLES 31:4–5

Up till then, they hadn't been given anything because they were corrupt. But when the righteous King Hezekiah took over, and God saw the people giving and doing what He said, He moved. God turned the spigot on so the people could get under the spout where the glory comes out. And when the glory of God fell on the nation of Israel, the Bible says they brought in abundance, their firstfruits. Notice how the Bible mentions *abundance* twice in that last verse. Then we see in verse 6:

> And concerning the children of Israel and Judah, that dwelt in the cities of Judah, they also brought in the tithe of oxen and sheep, and the tithe of holy things which were conse-crated unto the LORD their God, and laid them by heaps.
>
> —2 CHRONICLES 31:6

So much came in that they had literal *heaps* of the surplus. Now, watch what happens with the heaps. This is my favorite part of the whole story.

> In the third month they began to lay the foundation of the heaps, and finished them in the seventh month.
> —2 CHRONICLES 31:7

That's four months of offerings—money and valuable stuff that these people brought to the house of God and laid up in massive heaps. Can you imagine four months' worth of wealth piled up in heaps in the house of God? That's an amazing visual. Then we see, "And when Hezekiah and the princes came and saw the heaps, they blessed the LORD, and his people Israel. Then Hezekiah questioned the priests and the Levites concerning the heaps" (vv. 8–9). I bet he did. Here's the response:

> And Azariah the chief priest of the house of Zadok answered him, and said, Since the people began to bring the offerings into the house of the LORD, we have had enough to eat, and have left plenty: for the LORD hath blessed his people; and that which is left is this great store. Then Hezekiah commanded to prepare chambers in the house of the LORD; and they prepared them, and brought in the offerings and the tithes and the dedicated things faithfully: over which Cononiah the Levite was ruler, and Shimei his brother was the next.
> —2 CHRONICLES 31:10–12

When Hezekiah showed up at the house of God, he found so much abundance he had additional chambers constructed to keep the overflow until they could count through it all.

That's the result of obedience. It's important to note that the economy was terrible at the time, but still the people gave and gave and gave. Why? Because real revival always leads to real generosity.

THE PENTECOST AWAKENING

For our next biblical example, let's speed ahead into the New Testament to the Book of Acts. An event occurs fifty days after the resurrection of Jesus that we call Pentecost, which means "fifty." In the Old Testament, the number fifty was greatly significant in that every fiftieth year marked the year of Jubilee, which was the *year of release* when debts were forgiven and slaves were set free, as the presence of God would fall in unmistakable ways. Likewise, fifty days after the resurrection of Jesus, the glory of God fell like never before, thus beginning a New Testament Jubilee, as sins were forgiven and the people were set free by the grace of God.

As we look at Acts 2, Peter had just preached his most famous sermon, and three thousand people were saved and baptized, thereby establishing the Acts first-century church. Suddenly these new converts were learning the doctrine of the Scriptures while paying desperate and deep attention to what God was doing in their lives, so we see:

> And fear came upon every soul: and many wonders and signs were done by the apostles. And all that believed were together, and had all things common; and sold their possessions and goods, and parted them to all men, as every man had need.
>
> —ACTS 2:43–45

We've looked at the Too Much Revival and Hezekiah's Revival, and now we're going to look at the third revival in our review, the Pentecost Awakening—and what an awakening it was. This revival shook the people so radically that we still feel it today. Our church exists, and your church exists, and every other Christian church in the world exists because of the Pentecost Awakening. Pentecost was a onetime event. It will never be repeated, nor does it have to, because God left us the principles on how to experience the power of Pentecost, and these principles have been applied for nearly two thousand years.

As we learn from the record of Acts 2, the Holy Spirit shows up and shows out, and supernatural things start happening. Among these happenings are all the new converts who are suddenly and radically transformed. We're not talking about fifty-year-old believers who've had time to sit and think about it. We're talking about people who are brand-new to the faith. They had just come out of religion, and suddenly they were trusting in Jesus, despite the fact that most of them were going to have their heads cut off because of it. They didn't care, and those that survived gave up everything as they were driven underground.

You know what they did? They said, "You've got a need? And you've got a need? Oh, and you too? You also have a need? Well, I have this extra property. I have this extra boat. I have this extra bicycle. I have a little extra bling for the king. I have this cash in my pocket, some nice pottery out back, and some artwork I can fetch in Jerusalem and convert to money on eBay or Craigslist." You get the point.

The Bible says they sold their stuff, brought the proceeds to the church, and distributed it among the people to make sure everybody's bills got paid. That's God's welfare program, and it's the only such program there should be—the people of God taking care of the people of God. If we did that today, we would never need the government to help the poor, as the church would simply be the church. That is a lost art in the day and age in which we live, but make no mistake: it is a biblical command that the church has been disobeying for far too long.

Yet as we see in Acts 2, when revival came during the first century—when the Pentecost Awakening came—the people freely sold their possessions, and they gave to every man as he had need. I know a lot of folks reading this are thinking, "Well, that's sweet and all, but maybe that was just a one-and-done kind of event." But check this out. In Acts 4 we see:

> Neither was there any among them that lacked: for as many as were possessors of lands or houses sold them, and brought the prices of the things that were sold, and laid them down at the apostles' feet: and distribution was made unto every man according as he had need.
>
> —ACTS 4:34–35

Notice that in Acts 2 they only sold their possessions, but just two chapters later the people got so buck-wild generous that they began selling their houses and lands. They sold it all for the sake of those in need. They brought the money from the things sold and laid it down at the apostles' feet. And then they distributed it to every man according to his needs.

In all three of the biblical revivals we have studied, we see the same exact response. When the fire falls, the people can't help but give. They can't help but sacrifice. They sold their possessions, their lands, and their houses to make sure the church and the people were well taken care of.

WHAT'S WRONG WITH THIS PICTURE?

Today we in the church would not look at this scenario and say, "Wow, that's beautifully extravagant." No, instead we would say, "Wow, that's dangerously reckless."

I'm all for people enjoying nice things in moderation, so it's OK to have a little extra stuff. But in contrast, the people in these great revivals said, "We have what we need for our family. That family over there doesn't have much, so let's help them out. Let's sell that extra chariot and give the money to the church so they can help them." Imagine what could be done if we would get that mindset.

Looking back at the Pentecost Revival, when the people brought their money and laid it at the apostles' feet, take note that it wasn't because they worshipped the apostles. Not for one second. The apostles were simply the leaders of the church, so when they took up an offering, they were the ones who then distributed it all to the people.

The people trusted them because God trusted them first. If you cannot trust a leader with your money, you cannot trust them with your mind. If you cannot trust a pastor with resources, then you cannot trust him to teach you the truth of God's Word—nor can you trust him to be moral in any way.

When a man has money problems, he also has moral problems, and if God can't trust him with His resources, you shouldn't trust him as a church leader—until he repents and gets right with God (Gal. 6:1). The apostles are our role models for trustworthiness and morality, so the people had no trepidation about emptying into the storehouse that was the Acts church. The people understood that these apostles had biblical authority and were going to use the money correctly.

More people would be blessed with resources by churches all over America if the churches' money wasn't sitting in a bank for years. I can hear their leadership saying, "We can't give that kind of money away. We're putting it aside for a rainy day." They simply need to let God take care of the rainy days and drain that bank account to bless the people. That's the biblical model. If the church at large would obey the principles learned from the apostles of the Acts first-century church, can you imagine the difference it would make in our effort to reach the lost? If more pastors modeled Jesus and the apostles with their resources, can you imagine what that would do for the least and the hurting among us? If more churches obeyed God where giving is concerned, can you imagine the revival fires that would break out all around the world?

There is only one way to fix the financial disobedience of the modern local church. They need to start giving their money like crazy. It's the only way to lift the poverty spirit off a church and the best way to spark revival. You have to sow. You have to give and give and give. The original Christians of the Acts church literally sold all they had, brought their proceeds to the apostles, and said, "Whosoever has need in this church, please use this to take care of them." It worked, and church history is proof. Now it's our turn.

SPARKS OF REVIVAL TODAY

A dear friend of mine, Pastor Brian Gibson, has three church campuses that are all in full-blown revival. The biggest one is in Amarillo, Texas. While he drives and flies between them throughout the week, he has a great team of campus pastors that are loyal to him and keep the fires burning while he's away.

We hit the road together in 2020 and preached all over the country, sometimes as many as five times a day. Brian is the man who wrote the foreword in my book *Accessing Your Anointing*, as he was right there with me while I walked away from the cessationist theology of my seminary and my denomination, as is documented in that book and our documentary movie. Brian has been accessing his anointing for a very long time, so it's no surprise to me that he is seeing unbelievable generosity pouring out at all three of their campuses. For as we now know, radical generosity is always present when real revival breaks loose.

A lot of cattle ranchers go to Brian's church in Amarillo, and many of them are of big means, but nobody would ever know it. They are very humble people who never flaunt what they have.

Brian recently told me this story, and he started it by saying, "I've never seen anything like it in my life. I will be in the middle of my message, and somebody will walk up to the altar and just throw down a whole bag of silver and gold in the form of little bars and coins and bricks. Sometimes $20 worth, but we've seen upwards of $100,000 worth of gold at one time, just thrown onto the platform."

He continued, "I thought it was an anomaly, but then it started happening in every service. We had somebody that had two houses walk up to the platform to sign the title of the house over to the church. Another guy donated an airplane. What's a church going to do with an airplane?" Then he said, "From there, people started donating cars and trucks while the silver and gold continued pouring in. It was coming in heaps." Sound familiar? Brian went on to tell me how the church just started giving and giving and giving to everyone in need, yet still it's been difficult keeping up with it. Why? Because you simply can't out-give God. But you should try, so that's what they're doing.

These churches are remaining obedient in their tithes. They never forget that God owns it all, gives it all. They're sowing sacrificially, sometimes extravagantly. They're standing in faith that the Lord will keep His promises while faithfully participating in His kingdom economy—so they're reaping like crazy. And all the while, they have the reward of knowing that with every gift and sacrifice, they're storing up treasure in heaven. Don't ever forget what that implies.

So It Continues

Two or three weeks before finishing this book, Brian sent me a text that said, "Today we burned the note on our biggest building, and we are totally debt free as a church." That building seats about nine hundred people, and now suddenly it's paid in full—and they still have heaps left over. This is what happens when you have a house full of good and faithful servants who do not love or serve their money but only God. It's a beautiful sight to see.

At our Prophetic Conference here at Global Vision, Brian told one of his church's generosity stories to the crowd one night. The next day I walked into my office, and there was a guy sitting in there waiting for me. He said, "Pastor, God tore me up last night." I said, "Why is that?" He said, "Look, I'm all for the Joseph principle. I'm all for storing it up. So I've got some stuff stored up, but when Pastor Brian started talking about that silver and gold, I looked over at my wife, she nodded her head, and I knew what God wanted me to do." And I kid you not, that man handed me a box full of silver bars, bricks, and coins.

Then a couple of weeks ago, a family approached me while I was reading my Bible, and before long the man said, "Pastor, we don't have a lot. As a matter of fact, we've come to the church for benevolence before." I said, "That's all right. You do what you have to do when you have to do it. Don't you worry about that one bit. No shame in that game." Then he said, "I've got this bag I want to give you. It's the inheritance I got from my dad, and I already know what it's worth."

The bag was full of beautiful collector coins made of silver and gold—some of them old and some of them ancient—and silver bars as well. When revival happens, people just start freely giving their stuff for the work of the kingdom. They no longer suffer from attachment syndrome. Now they have a generosity syndrome. They're no longer hoarding stuff that's just sitting in their house doing nothing for anyone. They know they'll eventually get it back multiplied as they continue to participate in God's kingdom economy.

Folks who suffer from attachment syndrome need to realize that if they die today, people who generally don't even deserve it are going to fight and fuss and scuffle over it without ever truly blessing anyone with it when the dust settles. It would be far better to say, "I know somebody that has a need. Let me bless them with this now while I'm still able to give it freely."

A PAIR OF SHOES FOR THE KINGDOM

Before shifting gears, I want to share one more story from the revival going on at Brian's churches, as it speaks directly to God's amazing kingdom economy at the grassroots level. He told me about a twelve-year-old Hispanic boy who walked up to the front during his message and took off his shoes. He's the son of a single mother who goes to the church, and Brian has no clue as to the whereabouts of his daddy. Prophet Gustavo was there, so this young boy walked up to Gustavo, removed his shoes, and said, "Prophet, I want to give my shoes to the work of the Lord." What's most surprising about this is that they weren't even taking an offering, but there he was.

Speaking in his native tongue of Spanish, Gustavo asked, "You want to give your shoes in the offering?" And the boy said, "Yes, sir." Picture this kid sitting there barefoot as he gave his shoes to Gustavo. Suddenly the Holy Spirit spoke to Gustavo and told him to auction them off from the platform. So he held up the shoes in front of the congregation and obeyed.

This boy was sitting there barefoot because he didn't have anything else to give, even though it wasn't offering time. (But it's always offering time when you're paying attention!) In no time at all they raised about two grand for this kid's pair of shoes. Here's the kicker. Gustavo then stuffed all that cash into the shoes and gave them back to the boy with one instruction: "Take this to your mama."

At the end of the service, Brian approached some of his

cattle rancher brothers and said, "That single mama right there, let's make sure she never has another need until her boy turns eighteen and becomes a man." And the cattlemen were like, "Amen, Pastor, we will make sure of it." I'm tearing up while I'm writing this. Can you imagine? This beautiful transaction happened simply because a faithful boy felt the glory of God's presence, pulled off his shoes, and said, "I want to give to the house of God." Wow. Remember what Jesus said in Luke 6:38? "Give, and it shall be given unto you; good measure, pressed down, and shaken together, and running over, shall men give into your bosom."

Once again we see that you can't out-give God because you can't out-God God. When revival breaks out, God stirs the hearts of His people, and the people just start throwing stuff on the altars. They won't just be sitting around saying, "Oh my goodness, I can't believe he's talking about money again." When revival breaks out, people start saying, "Oh my goodness, why isn't he talking about money? I've got something that's about to burn a hole in my pocket. I've got to give it to the man of God before this service is done."

You cannot show me one single revival in the history of the world that didn't produce radical levels of biblical generosity. It always happens.

CHAPTER 15

REVIVAL OF THE HEART

Y OU'LL SEE A few parallels in the young boy's shoe story with the story we're about to read in the Bible. In case you're thinking this sort of revival can only happen among crowds in a church setting, let's see how Jesus taught it scaled down to a single individual. So far we've only discussed revivals that occur collectively in the body. Now we're going to look at a revival that happened within a single person—in a single heart.

In Mark 12 we have this unnamed lady that we call the widow, as she's the one that gave the now-famous widow's mite. Let's pause to understand the insignificance of such a paltry amount if this woman were to give it today. I have an actual two-thousand-year-old widow's mite in my office that is encapsulated in a little case. It's smaller than a dime, and if you studied it, you would think, "You couldn't buy the skin of a chicken nugget with that today." But can you imagine—since this passage was written nearly two millennia ago—how many times this event has been preached, taught, explored, and explained, and how many people have been convicted to give based on what she gave?

If God's mathematics are different—and they are—can you fathom what that widow's compounded interest in heaven has been over the last two thousand years, once you factor in how many lives she has changed just from that single act of giving? Can you imagine the compounded interest she is still earning in heaven right now, even as you read about her in this book? I really don't think you can. That single act has been talked about billions, if not trillions, of times. And here we are, two thousand years later, still talking about it and still being moved.

In Mark 12, Jesus had just talked about widows that get deceived and defamed by religious people. The Bible has a lot to say about that problem. But then Jesus turns the tide and talks about this one widow in particular:

> And he sat down opposite the treasury and watched the people putting money into the offering box. Many rich people put in large sums. And a poor widow came and put in two small copper coins, which make a penny. And he called his disciples to him and said to them, "Truly, I say to you, this poor widow has put in more than all those who are contributing to the offering box. For they all contributed out of their abundance, but she out of her poverty has put in everything she had, all she had to live on."
>
> —MARK 12:41–44, ESV

Though we've all heard the story of the widow's mite, my question is, Have we really? Have we really paid attention to the details of what Jesus tells us about this unnamed woman? As we properly study this widow's amazing act, I'm going to give you four principles of stewardship that we learn from this passage.

1. Jesus pays close attention to the money flow. Please stop thinking, "I just don't think preachers ought to make money such a big deal." Jesus made money an extraordinarily big deal. Look at our key passage, where we see, "And he sat down opposite the treasury." How do we know He pays attention to money? Because He sat down right next to the treasury to watch the money flow! It's not like He didn't have plenty of other options for where to sit that day. You need to realize this was happening in a specific portion of the courtyard of the temple, so He had to go out of His way to sit down beside the treasury box just to behold how the people gave.

From this we know that Jesus went to the temple that day for one particular reason—to sit down by the offering buckets and watch what people were putting in them. Why is Jesus so interested in money? Because it belongs to Him. He has an investment. Remember the law of possession? He owns it all, and He clearly cares how you use it. He wants to distribute it wisely to the correct people, and to do that He needs to know what each person gives.

Ultimately, Jesus pays attention to the flow of money because money is connected to your heart, just as we've discussed throughout this book. He's the one who taught us, "For where your treasure is, there your heart will be also" (Matt. 6:21). So He indeed pays attention.

2. Giving must *always* have a pure motivation. I say

"must always" because many times we give without pure motivation. We want to be seen. We want to be recognized. We want to be acclaimed. We want to get a certificate. And let me just say this: I'm not against you writing things off on your taxes, but if the only reason you give is so you can get a tax break, you're giving for the wrong reason.

Let me tell you something your CPA won't tell you. Most folks don't even come close to giving enough of a percentage for it to matter. It might look cute to put some digits in that box on your income tax return, but it doesn't reduce the taxes that most have to pay. Recognize the fact that when you give, you can indeed do it *wrongly*. You can do it angrily. You can do it grudgingly or out of necessity. You've got to give out of pure motivation.

As we continue, now we see what pure motivation looks like. "And there came a certain poor widow, and she threw in *two mites*, which make a farthing" (v. 42, emphasis added). He is giving us an understanding that what she gave didn't seem to be much, but look at what preceded this: "And many that were rich cast in *much*" (v. 41, emphasis added). So Jesus is comparing *much* with what we would think is little.

Jesus is saying that these people were giving with false motivation. They were giving so they could beat their chest because they were rich. There was no sacrifice in what they were giving. They just wanted to hear the *clink, clink, clink* in the box. They wanted to turn heads. They wanted to be seen. They wanted to put their check in the offering and hold it up high before dropping it in, as it were. They weren't giving *much* to lay up treasure in heaven; they were giving from their *much* so they could have more influence in the community.

Meanwhile, the Bible says this little woman came in—a

certain poor widow. Jesus wants us to be able to picture this poor, broke widow. Her husband's gone, and she's all alone to care for herself. Then she throws in "two mites, which make a farthing."

In our modern context, it's like saying, "She threw in two nickels that made a dime." The nickels or the dime didn't matter, because in both estimations it was not much, especially in comparison to what these rich guys just gave. But then notice something that we often miss, where we read, "And Jesus sat over against the treasury, and beheld *how* the people cast money into the treasury."

Did you catch that this time? It doesn't say He beheld *what* they put in, although He knew because He's God. It says He beheld *how* they did it. You see, giving has an attitude with it. Because giving is not just what we do, it's who we are, and Jesus was checking the motivation of their hearts. It wasn't *what* they were giving that was problematic. It was *how* they were giving and the underlying reason for their giving. We need to give with no expectations at all, other than to know God is going to bless us for simply being obedient. That's *how* we should give.

3. Sacrificial giving will always have a deep cost. That's why it's called sacrificial giving; it requires a sacrifice. As we continue in the story, we see, "He called unto him his disciples, and saith unto them, Verily I say unto you, that this poor widow hath cast more in, than all they which have cast into the treasury" (v. 43).

Some can read that and say, "How could Jesus say such a thing? These people were putting in some big bucks, and she put in two nickels. Yet He said, 'She gave more than all of them combined'?" But then Jesus answers them. *"For they all did cast in of their abundance; but she of her want did cast in all that she had, even all her living"* (v. 44, emphasis added). Her giving was at a level of sacrifice well beyond anything the other people gave. While they gave out of abundance, she gave out of poverty. They gave a fraction of their wealth and had much more still in the bank, while she gave everything she had to live on. No wonder she's the one we've been talking about for the last two thousand years. When you give out of your abundance, there is no sacrifice in it.

It would be like a guy walking up to the offering bucket and saying, "Here are the keys to my Porsche." Everybody would think, "Wow! Let's give him a brass plaque on the end of a pew with his name on it." But here's what they don't know: he owns a car lot. He's got tons of luxury vehicles, not just one. So it wasn't a sacrifice. It was giving out of abundance.

The widow, on the other hand, had no such abundance. The Bible says she gave out of her *want*. I like how the Bible is very specific. She probably *wanted* to keep that money to meet her very real and present needs. That's what it means. She needed it. She had bills to pay. She literally gave all that she had and was hoping God would come through for her next meal. Now, that's extravagant sacrificial giving.

She was probably thinking, "Whoa, I really need this money." But out of obedience to God, she quietly walked down, and—*kerplunk, kerplunk*—she gave all that she had. Meanwhile, the rich who cast in much probably looked over at Jesus thinking, "Did You see what I gave?" And Jesus would have said, "Yes, I saw that, and it cost you nothing. Next." As He stated on the record, "Verily I say unto you, that this poor widow hath cast more in, than all they which have cast into the treasury. For they all did cast in of their abundance; but she of her want did cast in all that she had, even all her living." She gave 100 percent of all she had.

This brings us to the fourth and final principle. I believe it's the most overlooked principle of stewardship, and it may reveal the reason why we have yet to be released into real biblical *revival* levels of generosity today.

4. God measures our giving by what we keep for ourselves. Man measures giving by what we give to others. God measures giving by what we keep for ourselves. The percentage we keep for ourselves is usually far higher than what we give away to other people. We know this fourth principle to be true and fundamental because Jesus said so right there in the text. She gave "more...than all" of them combined (v. 43). How is that so, Jesus? Because she gave everything she had to live on—that's 100 percent.

The number one reason people do not give extravagantly is because they fear they won't have enough left over for themselves. We think, "If I give to the work of God, I won't have enough to pay my bills." To that I say, "Really? Why would you say that when the Bible plainly says God will meet all your needs, and then some?" We either believe the Lord, or we don't.

ELIJAH AND THE WIDOW

Widows have always been important to the Lord, as they should be to all of us. In 1 Kings 17, it was the time of the great drought and famine that had swept the land, and the prophet Elijah was starving, so the Lord commanded him to go and find a woman who would provide food for him. As it turns out, this woman was a widow with a son, and they too were starving and down to their last small meal. Despite knowing this, Elijah simply obeyed God and asked her to fetch him something to drink. As she was heading to fetch a drink for the prophet, look what happened next:

> And as she was going to bring it, he called to her and said, "Bring me a morsel of bread in your hand." And she said, "As the LORD your God lives, I have nothing baked, only a handful of flour in a jar and a little oil in a jug. And now I am gathering a couple of sticks that I may go in and prepare it for myself and my son, that we may eat it and die."
> —1 KINGS 17:11–12, ESV

Can you imagine being in that situation? Talk about lack. The drought and famine had been killing folks all across the land, and this widow was down to her very last meal. Yet here was this wild prophet of God telling her to make sure she met his needs first.

> And Elijah said to her, "Do not fear; go and do as you have said. But first make me a little cake of it and bring it to me, and afterward make something for yourself and your son. For thus says the LORD, the God of Israel, 'The jar of flour shall not be spent, and the jug of oil shall not be empty, until the day that the LORD sends rain upon the earth.'"
> —1 KINGS 17:13–14, ESV

This woman just said, "Hey, man of God, we have hardly anything. Not only do we not have much, we have less than enough for our last meal. We're dying over here." And Elijah said, "That's cool. Don't worry about it. First make me a little cake and then scrape together something for you and your son from whatever's left over." How is that for audacity?

Surely she was thinking, "Did you not hear me? Make you one first?" But now look what happened:

> And she went and did as Elijah said. And she and he and her household ate for many days. The jar of flour was not spent, neither did the jug of oil become empty, according to the word of the LORD that he spoke by Elijah.
>
> —1 KINGS 17:15–16, ESV

This is a perfect example of the firstfruits principle, and for that, what you have is always enough to remain obedient. She wasn't ready for the blessing she had surely been praying for until she relinquished what little bit she still had. Like the widow who gave her last two mites, she trusted in the promises of God and just let it go. Once she did, *bam!* She, her son, the prophet of God, and all her workers ate for many days. God has a way of stretching what He puts in your hands if you'll simply give Him your firstfruits.

I hope you didn't miss the overflow of God's blessing, as the Lord restored the oil and the flour daily until the famine ended. He opened up the windows of heaven and poured out her blessing—pressed, down, shaken together, and running over.

THE DISHONEST STEWARD

In Luke 16 we find what I consider, hands-down, the most powerful explanation of biblical generosity in the whole Bible.

By saying that, you can assume it is also the most avoided and overlooked context, because most people read it and think, "I have no idea what that means, so I'm going to make up some silly application and just be done with it." I have to admit, it's probably the most challenging parable of them all.

I've even heard some seminary-trained preachers totally misinterpret its meaning in a public sermon.

For example, years ago when I first came across this passage, it really set me on fire for stewardship, and you'll see why in just a moment. While I was first developing this passage of Scripture for my own teaching, I was in Ohio at a pastors' conference and getting ready to preach to about seventy pastors. It was a great conference, until...

I was scheduled to be the last speaker that night, and because I was preaching to pastors, I wanted to talk about the levels of stewardship, so I was planning to preach from this passage of Scripture. Typically I don't even know what I'm going to preach on before I get there; I usually just jump and say, "OK, Lord, take over."

But this particular day was different, so I wondered, "Why does the Lord want me to preach this passage from Luke 16? It's such a hard passage to understand." Lo and behold, as I sat there waiting to preach, the pastor before me gets up and says, "I want you all to turn to Luke chapter 16, and I'm going to pick out a couple of words from the story." What he was really saying was, "I'm going to pick out a couple of words from this story because I don't even understand it myself, so I'm not going to take time to explain it to you."

I thought, "I'm going to have to get up there and clean up his mess," because I knew I was supposed to preach on that passage. Sure enough, it was a debacle of a sermon. I asked God, "Am I really going to have to get up and fix that?" And the Holy Spirit said, "Oh yeah, because I told you what to preach before he made up that mess."

There was literally nothing biblical about what he said. It was a cute little application at best, and at worst it was a theological nightmare. I said to myself, "These preachers are going to think I'm crazy." But I didn't care because the Lord lit a fire in those preachers that night. When I finished preaching, there was no doubt in my mind that everybody got it right the second time around. Praise God.

I'll be the first to recognize that the greatest commentary in the Bible is not from Greg Locke or Matthew Henry. It's from the Word itself. In Luke 16, we have the parable of all parables to prove that giving is not just something we do as an afterthought but is an eternal investment in the lives of others, and I'm going to prove it to you.

While I'm going to teach this parable in expository fashion—verse by verse and line by line—let's first read it in its entirety. When we get to Luke 16:1, Jesus has already been teaching a series of parables.

> He also said to the disciples, "There was a rich man who had a manager, and charges were brought to him that this man was wasting his possessions. And he called him and said to him, 'What is this that I hear about you? Turn in the account of your management, for you can no longer be manager.' And the manager said to himself, 'What shall I do, since my master is taking the management away from me? I am not strong enough to dig, and I am ashamed to beg. I have decided what to do, so that when I am removed from management, people may receive me into their houses.' So, summoning his master's debtors one by one, he said to the first, 'How much do you owe my master?' He said, 'A hundred measures of oil.' He said to him, 'Take your bill, and sit down quickly and write fifty.' Then he said to another, 'And how much do you owe?' He said, 'A hundred measures of wheat.' He said to him, 'Take your bill, and write eighty.' The master

commended the dishonest manager for his shrewdness. For the sons of this world are more shrewd in dealing with their own generation than the sons of light. And I tell you, make friends for yourselves by means of unrighteous wealth, so that when it fails they may receive you into the eternal dwellings."

—JESUS (LUKE 16:1–9, ESV)

CHAPTER 16

WE WILL GIVE
AN ACCOUNT

WHEN JESUS USES red letters in these *rich man* analogies, where He is talking about a ruler as a rich man who owns stuff, in the context He is referring to God the Father. In verse 1 of our parable, we see there was a rich man who had a steward that worked for him as would a financial assistant or CPA, someone who managed the books. We also see that the steward was accused of wasting his master's goods.

How he wasted the rich man's goods is not important, because the Bible does not denote how, but what it does denote is that he literally got caught red-handed cooking the books. So the steward was brought before the rich man.

In verse 2 we see the rich man asking, in effect, "How can I be hearing this? I've trusted you with my bank account, and you have absconded with my money. You've wasted it. You've mishandled it. You've misused it. You've lied and probably stolen it. Show me the books immediately." In the KJV it reads, "Give an account of thy stewardship."

You see that word *account*? It's also used in Romans 14, where the Bible says, "So then every one of us shall give *account* of himself to God" (v. 12). It's the same word in the Greek, *logos*, which means "a spoken word." Did you know that when you stand at the judgment seat of Christ, you are going to give a spoken account of what you did or did not do with the resources God placed in your hands according to this story? Don't miss that element of this parable.

But notice where the rich man said, "for thou mayest be no longer steward." In plain English, he just lost his job. And if you're a steward that works for a rich king, and you lose your job, you lose everything because you lived in his palace. Once you lose your job, you no longer have a place to live. You're going to be absolutely homeless. You mishandled the fortune that was given into your hands freely, and because of that you may no longer be steward. You have nothing. You are done. You have also forfeited your reward—which is a beautiful message in its lesson to us. You may be saved and going to heaven, but if you are not a good steward, you forfeit your reward when you get there. Nobody wants to talk about that reality, but it's in the Word.

So the king says, "You step down from your position and get out of my house. But before you leave, show me the books so I can determine your punishment." Which brings us to verse 3, where we see the steward start talking to himself as his wheels get turning. He basically says, "Man, what am I going to do? I lost my job. I got caught red-handed. I'm not going to be able to eat. I'm going to be homeless. What shall

I do?" Notice that he then says to himself, "I'm not strong enough to dig, and I'm too proud to beg."

What happens next is the most theologically fantastical verse in the whole Bible on stewardship, so watch what happens in verse 4, where he says, "I am resolved what to do, that, when I am put out of the stewardship, they may receive me into their houses." I know that's a weird line, so let me explain.

At the top of verse 5 we see, "So he called every one of his lord's debtors..." Let's pause and ask a question. Did these debtors owe *him* money? No. They owed his boss money. I'll let you in on his thinking. What he is about to do is leverage somebody else's resources (his boss's) to gain favor from others (the boss's debtors) that he does not deserve. They're not his resources; they belong to his boss, the rich man. But he is going to leverage them to gain influence and favor, nonetheless.

Now let's continue with verses 5–6, where we see, "So he called every one of his lord's debtors unto him, and said unto to the first, How much owest thou unto my lord? And he said, An hundred measures of oil. And he said unto him, Take thy bill, and sit down quickly, and write fifty."

Do you see what this guy just did? He found a man that owed his previous boss a hundred, and he said, "I want you to strike through that 100 and change it to 50." He gave the debtor a 50 percent discount on the spot, no questions asked. But he doesn't stop there.

In verse 7 we see, "Then said he to another, And how much owest thou? And he said, An hundred measures of wheat. And he said unto him, Take thy bill, and write fourscore." Which is 80, so he gave this debtor a 20 percent discount.

Let's review. He gives the first debtor a 50 percent discount, then he gives the next guy a 20 percent discount, and it's not even his money. He gives them both a little hug and says with a smile, "Now get out of here." By the way, don't you ever do this kind of thing. If you cook books like this, you'll go to prison.

We have to ask ourselves, Why in the world would this guy start offering discounts on books he doesn't even have responsibility for anymore? It's not his job, so why is he still working it? Remember when he said, "They may receive me into their houses"? Here's the plan he had cooked up in his mind: "If I can use my boss's money to gain favor with people I don't even know, once I get booted from the stewardship and kicked out of the palace, I can avoid being homeless. I'll just leverage these people's resources in a way that will make them feel compelled by gratitude to allow me to come into their houses."

He gave them all discounts, so they were going to feel obligated to have this man come into their homes and live rent-free. He used somebody else's money to gain favor he didn't even deserve, which in turn would make him welcome in a home that normally would have never welcomed him. Do you see the picture?

Then he did it again. I don't know why he gave a 50 percent discount to one and a 20 percent discount to the other, but it doesn't matter. The point is, now he didn't just have a place to stay; he also had an ace in the hole. So when he eventually gets the boot, both of these people will say within themselves, "Wow! I like that guy because he gave me a huge discount. If he needs a place to stay, I'm going to invite him into my house. He can stay in the basement for six months. I'll put him in the spare bedroom or maybe build him a little chamber. He earned it."

To review, the steward said in effect, "I'm going to use my boss's money to gain favor with people that owe me nothing. And by using his money, I'm going to gain favor with these people so I have a place to go, and they'll welcome me with open arms."

If that's not weird enough, things get even weirder in verse 8, where it says, "And the lord commended the unjust steward." That seems like a great contradiction, right? But it's not. This is where we have to remember that the rich man in the parable is referring to God. If it were a mere man, you would never expect such a response. But when we remember that we're talking about the holy God of heaven, it changes everything.

God commended an act that—in the natural economy and law of this world—would be one of the most illegal and unethical practices a man could commit. Yet it worked in the sight of the Lord. As He said, "Well, I'll be—I'm going to commend you for that, Son." Why? I'm glad you asked.

In verse 8 we see, "The lord commended the unjust steward, because he had done *wisely*" (emphasis added). This word *wisely*, in this context, is not speaking of biblical wisdom. Instead it means *shrewdly*. It's almost like saying, "Wow! That was slick." Now, we have to ask, how could Jesus justify commending somebody for doing something so unethical? I'll explain it to you like this.

THE ALCATRAZ METAPHOR

Have you ever been on the tour boat that visits Alcatraz Prison in San Francisco Bay? It's kind of an eerie, weird, ghostly type of place. You might know that I'm a bit of a history buff. I enjoy learning names and numbers and dates and facts and figures and all this info that most folks view as useless. A while back I was watching a history show about these guys that supposedly escaped from Alcatraz years ago, and because they apparently succeeded in this escape, Alcatraz was eventually shut down. You might remember that Clint Eastwood made a movie about this story.

Nobody knows for sure if the escape was actually successful because the men have never been seen since, and some say the reports of its success were just for the sake of making the movie. I don't have any idea if they really made it or not. But here's what I do know.

As I watched that program, I was in utter amazement. These guys were slick. They tied blue jeans in knots and used the air out of accordions to blow up pants to make floats. They created mannequins to fool the guards and got hair from various people and places to make wigs for them. They used simple posters to hide holes in their cell walls, and somehow all these crazy ideas and many more worked.

We are talking about some *Shawshank Redemption* stuff that really happened. Once they got beyond the wall, they had to climb over a barbed-wire fence and then jump off a forty-foot wall to splash into seawater that would have been about 20 degrees Fahrenheit. It's a fantastical story, and it's easy to say there's no way they survived. As I watched that show, it's not as if I was going, "Woohoo! Go crooks!" But I greatly admired how slick and shrewd they had to be to do it. That's the same context of our parable.

Jesus was not commending the steward for being unethical. He was commending his shrewdness. He was basically saying,

"Sir, I admire what you did for the sheer thought you put into it." He wasn't commending the criminal act but the wisdom it took to understand the dire state of his condition and exactly what it would take to get out of it.

Don't forget, the man used the king's money to gain favor he didn't deserve with people he did not know so that when he found himself homeless, he would be welcomed by those he helped. Let me tell you why this is so important.

In the back half of verse 8 we see a rebuke to the church, as Jesus says, "The children of this world are in their generation wiser than the children of light." He's basically saying it's a shame when lost people have more wisdom than church people. And it's also a shame that lost people understand how financial leverage works more than God's people do.

Then verse 9 brings it all together when He says, "And I say unto you, Make to yourselves friends of the mammon of unrighteousness." What? We already discussed what mammon is while studying Matthew 6. It's a Babylonian term that means materialism, money, stuff, wealth.

You might ask, "Did God just tell us to use money to make friends?" No. Let's read it again and this time to the end of the verse. He said, "Make to yourselves friends of the mammon of unrighteousness; that, when ye fail, they may receive you into everlasting habitations."

By the way, that's the phrase from Luke 16 that the preacher at the top of this discussion took out of context. He preached an entire sermon on *failure* from those three words: "when ye fail." Here's the problem with the way He misinterpreted the word *fail*.

When Jesus says, "Make to yourselves friends of the mammon of unrighteousness; that, when ye fail," the word *fail* in this context is the same word we use for heart failure, so Jesus is talking about death. He is not talking about tripping. He is not talking about moral decline. He is talking about dying.

As we bring this study to a close, it's about to get *real*, real quick. Jesus was saying in effect, "Greg Locke, everybody reading this book, I want you to make friends using unrighteous mammon—worldly money—so that when you die, the people you won using the mammon will welcome you into eternal habitations."

Here's what we know. The man in this parable that used someone else's resources to gain favor did not deserve that favor. But when he got kicked out—when he failed—the people he influenced with that money said, "Welcome. Welcome. Welcome."

In this often misunderstood parable, Jesus turned the tables on the church—on me, on you, and everybody else reading this book—by teaching us this: just as this man used his boss's money to gain influence and win friendships, "in like manner" I am called by God to use God's money to gain influence I don't deserve with people I do not know. By winning them, once I die, they will greet me with great joy in heaven and say, "Thank you for blessing me and investing in my life."

That is the core purpose of biblical stewardship. It's an investment into people's lives—and thereby their eternal lives—and it's always done with God's money, not our own, because everything we have is His.

I know the story seems strange, and it's no wonder the preacher who didn't understand it totally missed the point. But in the context, the steward—one of the "children of this world" as Jesus noted—had the wisdom to leverage the king's money to store treasure in heaven. That's the counterpoint of the rebuke Jesus makes to the church through this parable. Most of us in the church—"the children of light"—live as if the resources we have are all for us, so our love of money keeps us from leveraging it for the sake of others as God commands. Greed or fear (or both) dumb us down, so we miss the wisdom and shrewdness that even a lost criminal can muster up.

This steward, though wicked, was forced to focus on his ultimate destination. He had nothing to his name and nowhere to go, and he knew it, so his sudden eternal perspective brought him great wisdom, and that's what the church is lacking today. When it comes to our unrighteous money, most of us entirely ignore our ultimate destination. We never even consider our "eternal habitations," so we fail to leverage God's money to store treasure in heaven.

We saw where that ignorance can lead us through our study of the wicked servant in the parable of the talents from Matthew 25. We do not want his fate. In the end, the ones the Lord will commend by saying, "Well done, good and faithful servant," are the only stewards who leveraged His money for the eternal benefit of all.

WHAT IT SAYS TO ME

When I study this incredibly rich and mysterious parable, here's what God says to me: "Son, use My money to reach people with the gospel so that when you die, the people you reached with the gospel using My money will meet you in heaven and say, 'Welcome home, Greg Locke. Thank you for investing in my life.'" That's the purpose of stewardship in a nutshell and a legitimate example of treasure stored in heaven.

You can invest in people you never even shake hands with. You can support missionaries around the world. You may never meet them on earth. You may never meet those kids you helped. You may never meet the children you saved through the adoption foundation. You may never get a chance to meet those families you blessed.

You may never get on a jumbo jet and fly to Africa to preach a crusade with a million people, and you don't have to. You can support the people that do that. And do you know what you're doing when you're giving to your local church? You're not just haphazardly dropping a twenty on a plate to keep God and the preacher off your back. You're investing in the kingdom of God and storing treasure in heaven.

We simply have to change our perspective on money—from worldly to heavenly—because money is not the problem; it's the love of money that's the problem. If you love people, you will use money to reach people. But if you love money, you will use people to get more money.

REAL-WORLD APPLICATION

Just before we started Global Vision, about nineteen years ago, I was trying to get to Thailand for a preaching engagement when a businessman in Murfreesboro offered to help. I told him I had to go in two weeks so the ticket was going to be expensive, and I'd be gone for several weeks, so all my bills were going to become due. He said, "I'll tell you what, come to my office tomorrow."

When I got to his office, he said, "I'm in real estate, and I'm very successful, so I want to bless you with not only what you need to get to the mission field but also with funds to bless people while you're there and make sure you have no needs that go unmet while you're gone." He gave me this big check, and I headed off to Thailand.

While I was there preaching, hundreds of people got saved. The Holy Spirit showed up strong, and the glory of God fell. It was a beautiful sight. I preached in churches, orphanages, and every kind of event you could imagine. Today, this man is more successful than ever. God has abundantly blessed him.

Through me, he leveraged God's resources to gain influence with people he didn't know and will likely never meet on this side of glory—all because I was able to minister and bless these people on his nickel. When he dies, guess who is going to meet him at the judgment seat of Christ with a big, fat "Welcome home, and thank you for investing"? The people he reached using God's money.

That's the principle of investment. That's the principle of sowing and reaping. That's the principle of stewardship. When we support church planters and pastors and single moms and missionaries and evangelists, we are really investing in them and everyone else they will touch. We are leveraging the boss's resources, and we are gaining favor— storing up treasure—we don't even deserve.

No wonder Jesus told us that the world knows more about how money works than the church does. We'd better get busy reversing that. We'd better develop the giving savvy that Jesus is trying to teach us. Just like this real estate businessman, you don't have to be unethical; you just have to be shrewd with God's money, just as Jesus instructs. If you do that, one day you'll hear people say, "Thank you for what you gave to that local church! Thank you for what you did for that single mom! Thank you for what you did for that pastor! Thank you for what you did for that missionary's wife. Thank you for paying for that person's international travel so they could share the gospel! I've never met you, but let me hug you and welcome you to the kingdom of God." That's the result of good stewardship. That's what generosity is to Jesus. It's an investment in the kingdom.

You can pray and fast until the cows come home, but if you don't learn to be generous, you won't learn anything from praying and fasting. You'll just say a bunch of cute words and starve yourself. You can go to every church in town and get baptized in every river, but if you don't put into action what God is teaching you about money, you're no better than the Pharisees of old.

There's so much more in the Bible about money and generosity that we could discuss, but I think we're landing on the right note, so I'm going to close with a definition I heard years ago when I was in Bible college. An African missionary named Daryl Champion came to speak to us, and he began to tell witch doctor stories, which was odd, because Baptists weren't supposed to believe in that kind of stuff, and this was a Baptist seminary. He shared some demon stories that would make your hair stand up, and back then I didn't know anything about the power in the name of Jesus. This guy saw demons and witch doctors flying around, and he fought hell by the acres to stop them.

Champion was a little old, unassuming man, and he's in heaven now. My friends and I were true students of the Word, so we were eating up his stories like Skittles and M&Ms—we just couldn't get enough. As he got toward the end of his message, he said, "Let me tell you what real compassion is." Then he said, "Write this down." I will never forget what he did next. He loosened the knot on his tie and moved his glasses down a bit, leaned over, and said: "Compassion is love with shoes on." He was right, and I never forgot it.

The American church talks about compassion, but we've never put on our compassion shoes. Real compassion is not *telling* people we love them. It's *showing* them we love them, and according to the Bible, our love is only proven by our giving. We can sacrifice our time, our tears, our talents, our tithes, our treasure, and a thousand other T's you can think of, and it all matters to God, but talk is cheap. Real compassion is not what I can say in a microphone. Real compassion is when we get off the platform and get our hands dirty. We put our compassion shoes on, and we walk it out.

I'm going to close this chapter of my generosity journey where it began, reflecting back to that day when I was eighteen years old, sitting in Mexico, hearing the phrase that built me into everything I am today as a man: "There is nothing that will change your life more than biblical generosity."

Amen.

NOTES

CHAPTER 4

1. "Unlocking the Power of Giving in 2023: Church Donation Key Stats," Overflow, May 31, 2023, https://www.overflow. co/blog/unlocking-the-power-of-giving-in-2023-church-donation-key-stats.

CHAPTER 5

1. Skip Heitzig, "The Generous Lives of True Believers—Acts 2; 2 Corinthians 9," sermon, Calvary Church, January 27, 2019, Connect With Skip Heitzig, http://skipheitzig.com/teachings_view.asp?ServiceID=4379&detailednotes=0&relatedmessages=0&transcript=1&print=1.
2. "Our History," LeTourneau Christian Center, accessed June 18, 2024, https://www.letcc.org/about/our-history/.

CHAPTER 6

1. "Poverty and Shared Prosperity 2022," World Bank Group, accessed April 30, 2024, https://openknowledge.worldbank. org/server/api/core/bitstreams/b96b361a-a806-5567-8e8a-b14392e11fa0/content.

ABOUT THE AUTHOR

GREG LOCKE IS the founding and lead pastor of Global Vision Bible Church in Mount Juliet, Tennessee, just outside Nashville. He is the producer of the film *Come Out in Jesus Name* and host of the top-rated podcast *On Point With Pastor Greg Locke*. With a bachelor's degree in biblical studies and a master's degree in revival history, Locke is a revivalist and popular speaker in churches and political circles alike. He has achieved one of the largest social media platforms in the nation, and Global Vision has one of the broadest-reaching live stream ministries in the world. Locke and his wife, Taisha, work hand in hand in the ministry, seeking to reach those who are oppressed and forgotten by the church. They share six children and one grandchild.

Find us at LockeMedia.org.

Global Vision Press ™

My FREE GIFT to You

DEAR READER,

God loves a giving soul. I sincerely hope that your journey through my book helped you not only enrich your mind with the knowledge and understanding about the power of generosity from a biblical standpoint but also gain a full confidence that our God will take what you give Him and do exceedingly and abundantly more than you could have asked for or imagined with it.

As my way of spreading the generosity, I am offering the eBook version of *Accessing Your Anointing* to you today for FREE!

To grab your gift, please go to:

MyCharismaShop.com/pages/generosity-journey-gift

God Bless Your Generous Soul,

Greg Locke

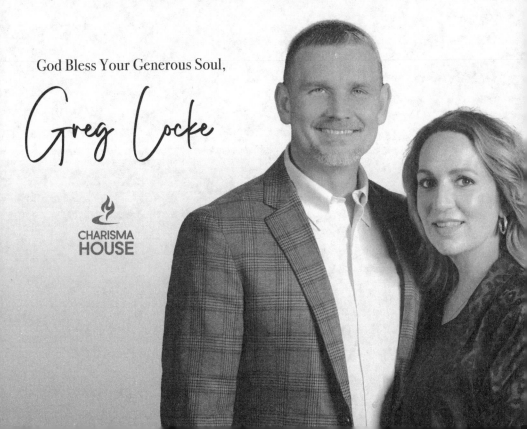

CHARISMA
HOUSE